SWEET & SAVORY

FAT BOMBS

100 Delicious Treats for Fat Fasts, Ketogenic, Paleo, and Low-Carb Diets

Martina Slajerova

FAIR WINDS

Quarto is the authority on a wide range of topics.

Quarto educates, entertains and enriches the lives of our readers—enthusiasts and lovers of hands-on living.

www.QuartoKnows.com

First published in the United States of America in 2016 by
Fair Winds Press, an imprint of
Quarto Publishing Group USA Inc.
100 Cummings Center
Suite 406-L
Beverly, Massachusetts 01915-6101
Telephone: (978) 282-9590
Fax: (978) 283-2742
QuartoKnows.com
Visit our blogs at QuartoKnows.com

20 19 18 17 16   2 3 4 5

ISBN: 978-1-59233-728-6

Digital edition published in 2016
eISBN: 978-1-63159-172-3

Library of Congress Cataloging-in-Publication Data available.

Design: Burge Agency
Cover Image: Martina Slajerova
Photography: Martina Slajerova

Printed in China

The information in this book is for educational purposes only. It is not intended to replace the advice of a physician or medical practitioner. Please see your health-care provider before beginning any new health program.

I'd like to thank my parents for allowing me to follow my ambitions and my fiancé Nikos for believing in me.

I would also like to dedicate this book to Hana, my best childhood friend, who recently passed away. Thank you for being in my life. I am so lucky that you were my friend.

Contents

Introduction

It's been four years since I decided to cut out sugar, grains, and processed foods from my diet. Here's why: Even though I ate well and exercised regularly, I suffered constantly from fatigue and other issues and, in 2011, I was diagnosed with Hashimoto's hypothyroidism, an autoimmune disease. My doctor prescribed medication, but that didn't help with some of the symptoms I was experiencing. Plus, maintaining a healthy weight proved to be a huge challenge, and even though I was sleeping more than 9 hours each night, I had zero energy.

Finally, I decided to do my own research and, like many other health-conscious folks, I started following a low-carb, primal diet. I haven't looked back since. I feel better than ever and, for the first time in my life, I don't feel like I'm dieting all the time. I have more energy; I exercise less than I used to, and still manage to maintain a healthy weight.

Quitting sugar and grains wasn't easy at first, but once I survived the first three or four weeks—which were mainly devoted to recovering from my "sugar hangover"—I realized how easy it was to avoid carbs. I was also delighted that I was able to enjoy delicious, nutritious foods that I used to think were unhealthy—and that I finally got my health condition under control. What I realized is, once you make the decision to go low-carb—and commit to it—you'll soon stop missing sugar and grains, and you'll enjoy eating whole foods without being plagued by cravings.

Don't get me wrong: I love treats and snacks just like anyone else! Luckily, there's a healthy, low-carb way to enjoy truffles, ice cream, and even chocolate bars. And that's where this book comes in. My previous cookbook, *The KetoDiet Cookbook* (2015), features more than 150 low-carb recipes suitable for everyday cooking on a ketogenic diet—but this book will show you how to make more than 100 recipes for sweet treats and filling, savory snacks (plus quick meal ideas that won't spike your blood sugar). But first, what is the KetoDiet, and why is it a good idea to eat more healthy fats and fewer carbs?

Chapter 1

The KetoDiet in a Nutshell

A ketogenic diet is a type of low-carbohydrate diet that's high in fat, moderate in protein, and low in carbs. Typically, the macronutrient ratio in terms of calories sits within the following ranges:

✻ 60 to 75 percent (or even more) of calories from fat

✻ 15 to 30 percent of calories from protein

✻ 5 to 10 percent of calories from carbs

To follow a low-carb, ketogenic diet, you can limit either your total carb intake or your net carb intake. Net carbs are total carbs without fiber.

Since the KetoDiet is a high-fat diet, most of your daily energy intake should come from fats. Increasing your fat intake and cutting carbohydrates lead to a beneficial metabolic state called *ketosis*. Ketosis causes the liver to produce ketone bodies, which shift the body's metabolism away from using glucose as the main energy source and encourage it to utilize fat instead. Simply put, this means your body will burn fat instead of sugar, and it'll learn to use ketones and fat as its primary sources of energy.

Switching to fat as your primary energy source has lots of benefits. First of all, when you eat fewer carbs (50 grams or less of total carbs a day), you'll experience fewer cravings and will naturally eat less. Second, with adequate protein intake, a ketogenic diet enhances your ability to build and preserve muscle tissue. Finally, carb restriction is not only beneficial for weight management, but also has myriad health benefits. Several clinical trials have shown that low-carb diets can improve health conditions such as diabetes, Alzheimer's, epilepsy, and even cancer.

That said, it's not just how much fat and protein you consume that matters. Food quality plays a major role in weight management and in your overall well-being. When you increase your fat intake on a low-carb diet, always opt for these healthy fats:

* Saturated fats (lard, tallow, chicken fat, duck fat, goose fat, clarified butter/ghee, butter, coconut oil). Saturated fats have gained a bad reputation over the years, but recent studies—such as a meta-analysis published in the January 2010 issue of *The American Journal of Clinical Nutrition*—show no link between the consumption of saturated fats and coronary heart disease. Saturated fats are the most stable fats; their high smoke points make them perfect for cooking.

* Monounsaturated fats, also known as "heart-healthy" fats (avocado, macadamia, and olive oil).

* Polyunsaturated fatty acids, especially omega-3s from animal sources (fatty fish and seafood). Both omega-3 and omega-6 fatty acids are essential, which means our bodies cannot synthesize them, so we need to get them from foods we eat. Studies show that most people are deficient in omega-3 fatty acids but consume too much of the omega-6 variety. The aim is to balance your omega-6-to-omega-3 ratio.

And *avoid* these unhealthy fats at all costs:

* Refined fats and oils (e.g., sunflower, safflower, cottonseed, canola, soybean, grapeseed, corn oil)

* Trans fats, such as margarine

Why Fat Bombs?

It's not surprising that most people think of greasy junk food when they hear the phrase "fat bombs." In most people's minds, a fat bomb looks like a large bowl of ice cream topped with syrup, a candy bar, or a burger and fries from the fast-food restaurant down the street. But, within the context of a low-carb diet, the term "fat bomb" has a completely different—and much healthier—meaning.

If you're on a low-carb diet, ensuring that your diet contains enough healthy fats can be tricky, especially if you're new to this way of eating. That's where fat bombs come in: high in fat and low in protein and carbohydrates, they're the ideal snacks if you're eating low carb.

While most fat bombs should be used as occasional treats—not meal replacements—there are exceptions to the rule. Some recipes can be used as complete meals (I've indicated where this is the case throughout this book). Here's how to include fat bombs in your diet:

* Use them to boost your fat intake to meet your macronutrient targets. At least 80 percent of the calories in the recipes in this cookbook come from fats, which makes them ideal when you need to boost your fat intake without exceeding your protein and carb targets.

* Enjoy a fat bomb when you don't have time to cook and need a quick hit of energy.

* Use them as pre- or post-workout snacks instead of "regular" snacks that are high in carbs.

* Try fat bombs if you're on a fat fast (together with other foods suitable for this diet plan).

Essential Fat Bomb Ingredients

Here are some of the essential ingredients for making fat bombs:

Nuts

Seeds

Coconut

Coconut oil

Cacao butter

Full-fat dairy

Activated Nuts and Seeds

Activated nuts and seeds (think: soaking or sprouting) are best because they're more easily digested, and their nutrients are better absorbed. Roasting also helps reduce the levels of phytic acid, which inhibits the absorption of nutrients during digestion, but soaking nuts first is more effective. Additionally, soaking and drying them produces a crunchier texture and more delicious flavor.

Soaking nuts is simple. Place them in a bowl filled with water or salted water and leave at room temperature overnight. Drain and spread on a parchment-lined baking sheet and place in the oven or a dehydrator for 12 to 24 hours, turning occasionally, until completely dry. See the sidebar on the next page for dehydrating temperatures. Store in an airtight container.

Coconut Products

Desiccated coconut is shredded and dehydrated coconut meat. Always use the unsweetened variety.

Coconut flour is a finely ground flour made from coconut meat from which the oil has been removed.

Coconut butter is made from dehydrated coconut meat in the same way nut and seed butters are made.

Coconut milk is the liquid extracted from the grated meat of a coconut. (It should not be confused with coconut water.) It may contain as much fat as heavy whipping cream. You can also find it in its dehydrated form as coconut milk powder.

Creamed coconut milk or coconut cream is the fatty part of coconut milk that has been separated from the watery part. If a recipe calls for creamed coconut milk, make it a day ahead. To "cream" coconut milk, simply place the can in the refrigerator overnight. The next day, open the can, spoon out the solidified coconut milk, and discard the liquids. Do not shake the can before opening. One 14-ounce (400 g) can will yield about 7 ounces (200 g) of coconut cream.

Coconut oil is fat extracted from the meat of mature coconuts. It's high in saturated fatty acids and easily digestible medium-chain triglycerides

(MCTs). Keep in mind that coconut oil melts at room temperature and any treats made with it should be refrigerated.

Cacao and Chocolate

Cacao butter or cocoa butter is pure fat extracted from cacao beans. It has a high smoke point and long shelf life, and consists of mostly saturated and monounsaturated fatty acids. Unlike coconut oil, it stays solid at room temperature.

Cacao paste—also known as cacao liquor or unsweetened chocolate—is pure cocoa mass and becomes liquid when heated. It contains both cacao solids and cacao butter.

Cacao powder is often referred to as *cocoa*, but technically, raw cacao powder is made from raw cacao mass, while cocoa powder is made from roasted cacao and may also contain added sugar, milk fats, or oils. Make sure to choose a sugar-free version!

Cacao nibs are cacao beans that have been roasted, separated from their husks, and crushed into smaller pieces. They are sometimes confused with dark chocolate chips—but unlike dark chocolate, cacao nibs don't contain any sugar.

Dark chocolate or bittersweet chocolate is made with a minimum of 70 percent cacao solids. Personally, I never use chocolate with less than 85 to 90 percent cacao solids. The more cacao, the less sugar it contains—which means it'll cause fewer cravings!

Dairy and Dairy Substitutes

I use butter, cream cheese, heavy cream, and mascarpone cheese to make some of the fat bombs in this book, but I've also included dairy-free alternatives in most recipes.

What Is a Fat Fast?

When you begin a ketogenic diet, it will take 3 to 4 weeks for your body to start using ketones effectively for energy. Before you get keto-adapted, your main source of energy is glucose. A fat fast is a type of fasting that's suitable for those who reach a weight loss plateau when they're already keto-adapted. During a fat fast, you get about 80 to 90 percent of your calories from healthy fats while keeping your calorie intake low, no more than 1000 to 1200 kcal (kilocalories) a day. A fat fast should last no more than 3 to 5 days: any longer, and you risk sending your body into starvation mode, losing muscle, and becoming deficient in essential nutrients.

Find out more about fat fasts and the ketogenic diet on my blog: www.ketodietapp.com/blog.

How Long Should I Soak My Favorite Nuts and Seeds?

Almonds: soak for 8 to 12 hours; dehydrate at 120°F to 150°F (50°C to 65°C)

Hazelnuts: soak for 8 to 12 hours; dehydrate at 120°F to 150°F (50°C to 65°C)

Pine nuts: soak for 4 to 8 hours; dehydrate at 120°F to 150°F (50°C to 65°C)

Walnuts: soak for 4 to 8 hours; dehydrate at 120°F to 150°F (50°C to 65°C)

Pecans: soak for 4 to 8 hours; dehydrate at 120°F to 150°F (50°C to 65°C)

Brazil nuts: soak for 4 to 8 hours; dehydrate at 120°F to 150°F (50°C to 65°C)

Macadamia nuts: soak for 4 to 8 hours; dehydrate at 120°F to 150°F (50°C to 65°C)

Cashews: soak for 2 to 3 hours; dehydrate at 200°F to 250°F (90°C to 120°C)

Pistachios: soak for 2 to 3 hours; dehydrate at 200°F to 250°F (90°C to 120°C)

To sum it up:

* If a recipe calls for cream cheese or mascarpone, you can use creamed coconut milk instead.
* If a recipe calls for heavy whipping cream, use regular (liquid) coconut milk instead.
* If a recipe calls for butter, use coconut oil or ghee instead.

Sweeteners

In my experience, stevia, erythritol, and Swerve are the best natural low-carb sweeteners, and I've been using them in my cookbooks and on my blog for several years. The amount of sweeteners you use in your recipes depends on your palate. I don't use large amounts of sweeteners in the recipes in this book, so you may need to add a few extra drops of stevia or a little more erythritol to suit your palate. While erythritol and Swerve have about 70 percent of the sweetness of table sugar, pure stevia is 200 to 300 times sweeter than sugar—so use very small amounts to avoid a bitter aftertaste. If you're using liquid stevia, use no more than 3 to 5 drops per serving.

Apart from liquid stevia, there are other types of stevia-based sweeteners that you can use. While granulated products that usually contain both erythritol and stevia tend to be about as sweet as sugar, pure powdered stevia is as powerfully sweet as it is in its liquid form. Keep in mind the following conversions:

1 cup (200 g/7.1 oz) of granulated stevia = 1 teaspoon of powdered or liquid stevia

1 tablespoon (10 g/0.4 oz) of sugar = 6 to 9 drops of liquid or ¼ teaspoon of powdered stevia

1 teaspoon of sugar = 2 to 4 drops of liquid or a pinch of powdered stevia

Raw Eggs

Some recipes in this book call for raw eggs. If you're concerned about the potential risk of salmonella, use pasteurized eggs to make the recipe safer. To pasteurize eggs at home, simply pour enough water in a saucepan to cover the eggs. Heat to about 140°F (60°C). With a spoon, slowly lower the eggs into the saucepan. Keep the eggs in the water for about 3 minutes. This should be enough to pasteurize them, killing any potential bacteria. Let the eggs cool. They will keep, refrigerated, for 6 to 8 weeks.

Other Ingredients

Vanilla: If a recipe calls for vanilla, use either sugar-free vanilla extract or natural vanilla powder, which is made from the seeds of vanilla beans.

Freeze-dried berries, berry powder, and beetroot powder: Some recipes call for freeze-dried berry powder or beetroot powder. You can find unsweetened berry and beetroot powders in most health food stores and online.

Matcha: This is finely ground green tea powder. It's high in antioxidants and can boost your metabolism. Make sure you use unsweetened matcha powder.

Spices and herbs: These boost flavor or add color. Just like sweeteners, they should be used to taste, depending on your palate.

Making Fat Bombs

When you're sourcing ingredients, try to find them in their most natural forms—that is, organically grown and free from unnecessary additives. Buy organic eggs, organic unwaxed lemons, grass-fed butter, outdoor-reared pork, wild-caught fish, and extra-virgin coconut oil.

Also, when preparing the recipes from this book, keep in mind:

* All recipes in this book are well suited to the ketogenic, paleo, and primal diets. Several recipes also include dairy-free options.

* Nutritional values for each recipe are per serving unless stated otherwise. The nutritional data are derived from the USDA National Nutrient Database: http://ndb.nal.usda.gov.

* Nutritional facts are calculated from edible parts. For example, if one avocado listed is 7.1 ounces (200 g), this value represents its edible parts (seeds and peel removed) unless otherwise specified.

* Optional ingredients and suggestions are *not* included in the nutritional information.

A Note About Measurements

If you are following a ketogenic diet for specific health reasons, you should be aware that accuracy is vital for this diet to work. When measuring ingredients, always weigh them using a kitchen scale. Using measures like cups or tablespoons can lead to inaccuracies that may impact the macronutrient composition of your meal. All it takes to shift your body out of ketosis is a few extra grams of carbohydrates. Furthermore, cups and tablespoons for dried products (coconut flour, almond flour, etc.) may vary depending on the brand. Using a less-than-precise amount of an ingredient will affect the quality of a recipe and the final result will be less than desirable.

Chapter 2

The Basics

Before you start creating fat bombs, you'll need to make a few simple-to-prepare, basic ingredients, like nut and seed butters and homemade chocolate. Most nut and seed butters can be kept at room temperature for a few days, and will last for several weeks in a sealed glass jar in the refrigerator. You can also freeze nut and seed butters for 3 to 4 months. Homemade chocolate will keep refrigerated for up to 3 months. And, the best part is, all recipes are low-carb, sugar-free, and paleo friendly.

Almond and Cashew Butter

This delicious spread is a great paleo alternative to peanut butter.

Ingredients

1 cup (150 g/5.3 oz) almonds, blanched or whole

⅓ cup (50 g/1.8 oz) cashews

4 tablespoons (60 ml/2 fl oz) almond oil or macadamia nut oil

Pinch salt (optional)

Seeds from 1 vanilla bean (optional)

½ teaspoon ground cinnamon (optional)

Instructions

Preheat the oven to 350°F (175°C, or gas mark 4). Spread the almonds and cashews on a baking sheet and place in the preheated oven for 12 to 15 minutes. Watch carefully to prevent burning. Remove from the oven and cool.

In a food processor, pulse the nuts until smooth (or reserve some chopped nuts to add later for a chunkier texture). Depending on your processor, this may take some time. At first, the mixture will be dry. Scrape down the sides several times with a rubber spatula if the mixture sticks.

Add the oil. Continue to blend until you reach the desired consistency. The oil makes the butter smoother and more suitable for creating fat bombs. Add the salt and vanilla bean seeds or cinnamon (if using) and pulse to combine. Spoon the butter into a glass container. Seal and store at room temperature for up to 1 week or refrigerate for up to 3 months.

Nutrition facts per serving (2 tablespoons [32 g/1.1 oz]):

Total carbs:	Fiber:	Net carbs:	Protein:	Fat:	Energy:	Calories from:
5.5 g	**2.1 g**	**3.4 g**	**5.2 g**	**19.4 g**	**205 kcal**	**Carbs (6%)** **Protein (10%)** **Fat (84%)**

Yield:
**About 1 cup
(250 g/8.8 oz)**

Hands-on time:
10 mins

Overall time:
10 mins

Coconut and Pecan Butter

Keep a napkin handy. You'll drool over this cinnamon-spiced nut butter. Made with pecans and coconut, it's perfect for making chocolate treats.

Ingredients

2 cups (150 g/5.3 oz) dried shredded or flaked coconut

1 cup (100 g/3.5 oz) pecans

1 teaspoon sugar-free vanilla extract or ½ teaspoon vanilla powder

1 teaspoon ground cinnamon

¼ teaspoon salt

Instructions

In a food processor, combine the coconut, pecans, vanilla, cinnamon, and salt. Pulse until smooth and creamy. Depending on your processor, this may take a few minutes. At first, the mixture will be dry. Scrape down the sides several times with a rubber spatula if the mixture sticks.

Spoon the butter into a glass container. Seal and store at room temperature for up to 1 week or refrigerate for up to 3 months.

Nutrition facts per serving (2 tablespoons [32 g/1.1 oz]):

Total carbs:	Fiber:	Net carbs:	Protein:	Fat:	Energy:	Calories from:
6.5 g	4.4 g	2.1 g	5 g	11.6 g	154 kcal	Carbs (6%) Protein (15%) Fat (79%)

Yield:
**About 1 cup
(250 g/8.8 oz)**

Hands-on time:
5 mins

Overall time:
5–10 mins

Tip
To enhance this butter's flavor, use roasted pecans and coconut: Preheat the oven to 350°F (175°C, or gas mark 4). Spread the coconut and pecans on a baking sheet. Place in the preheated oven and roast for 5 to 8 minutes, or until the coconut is lightly golden. Stir once or twice to prevent burning.

Chocolate-Hazelnut Butter

This healthy, low-carb alternative to Nutella is just the thing for making truffles and it's also great in smoothies.

Ingredients

1 cup (150 g/5.3 oz) hazelnuts

1 cup (130 g/4.6 oz) macadamia nuts

½ cup (75 g/2.6 oz) almonds

1 bar (100 g/3.5 oz) extra-dark chocolate, 85 percent cacao or more

1 tablespoon (15 g/0.5 oz) coconut oil

1 tablespoon (5 g/0.2 oz) unsweetened cacao powder

1 teaspoon sugar-free vanilla extract or ½ teaspoon vanilla powder

2 tablespoons (20 g/0.7 oz) powdered erythritol (see Tip) or Swerve

Few drops liquid stevia, to taste (optional)

½ cup (120 ml/4 fl oz) coconut milk or heavy whipping cream (optional)

Instructions

Preheat the oven to 375°F (190°C, or gas mark 5). Spread the hazelnuts, macadamia nuts, and almonds on a baking sheet. Place in the preheated oven and bake for about 10 minutes, or until lightly browned. Remove the nuts from the oven and cool for 15 minutes.

Meanwhile, melt the dark chocolate and coconut oil in a double boiler, or heat-proof bowl placed over a small pot filled with 1 cup of boiling water, making sure the water doesn't touch the bottom of the bowl. Stir until melted.

Rub the hazelnuts together in your hands to remove the skins. This makes the butter smooth and avoids the bitter taste imparted by the skins. Place all of the nuts into a food processor and pulse until smooth.

Add the cacao powder, vanilla, erythritol or Swerve, and stevia (if using) to the melted chocolate. Pour the mixture into the processor with the nuts and pulse until smooth. If you're using coconut milk, add it to the processor and pulse again.

Transfer the butter to a glass container. Seal and refrigerate for up to 4 weeks if using coconut milk or 1 week using cream.

Nutrition facts per serving (2 tablespoons [32 g/1.1 oz])

Total carbs:	Fiber:	Net carbs:	Protein:	Fat:	Energy:	Calories from:
5.9 g	2.9 g	3 g	3.9 g	18.7 g	193 kcal	Carbs (6%) Protein (8%) Fat (86%)

Yield:
**About 2 cups
(500 g/1.1 lbs)**

Hands-on time:
5 mins

Overall time:
25 to 35 mins

Tip
To powder the erythritol, place it in a clean blender or coffee grinder and pulse until powdery, about 15 to 20 seconds.

| Yield: **1¼ cups (290 g/10.2 oz)** | Hands-on time: **5 mins** | Overall time: **10 mins** |

Eggnog-Macadamia Butter

Enjoy the flavors of the holiday season all year 'round! This macadamia-based butter is lightly spiced, creamy, and addictive.

Ingredients

2 cups (260 g/9.2 oz) macadamia nuts

1 teaspoon ground nutmeg

½ teaspoon sugar-free vanilla extract or ¼ teaspoon vanilla powder

½ teaspoon ground cinnamon

1 teaspoon sugar-free rum extract or 2 tablespoons (30 ml/1 fl oz) dark rum

2 tablespoons (20 g/0.8 oz) powdered erythritol or Swerve

Few drops liquid stevia, to taste (optional)

Instructions

In a food processor, combine the macadamia nuts, nutmeg, vanilla, cinnamon, rum extract or rum, and erythritol or Swerve. Add the stevia (if using). Process until smooth. The exact amount of time depends on your processor. Spoon the butter into a glass container. Seal and store at room temperature for up to 1 week or refrigerate for up to 3 months.

Nutrition facts per serving (2 tablespoons [32 g/1.1 oz])

Total carbs:	Fiber:	Net carbs:	Protein:	Fat:	Energy:	Calories from:
4.6 g	**2.8 g**	**1.8 g**	**2.3 g**	**21.7 g**	**209 kcal**	**Carbs (3%)** **Protein (4%)** **Fat (93%)**

Yield:	Hands-on time:	Overall time:
1²/₃ cups	**5 mins**	**10 mins**
(410 g/14.5 oz)		

White Chocolate and Macadamia Butter

This recipe combines some of the healthiest high-fat foods in a single jar of goodness: macadamia nuts, coconut butter, and cacao butter. The result? A white chocolate treat that's good for you, too.

Ingredients

1 cup (130 g/4.7 oz) macadamia nuts

½ cup (125 g/4.4 oz) coconut butter

½ cup (110 g/3.9 oz) cacao butter

2 teaspoons sugar-free vanilla extract or 1 teaspoon vanilla powder

¼ cup (40 g/1.4 oz) powdered erythritol or Swerve

Few drops liquid stevia, to taste (optional)

Instructions

In a food processor, combine the macadamia nuts, coconut butter, cacao butter, vanilla, and erythritol or Swerve. Add the stevia (if using), and process until smooth. The exact amount of time depends on your processor. Spoon the butter into a glass container. Seal and store at room temperature for up to 1 week or refrigerate for up to 3 months.

Nutrition facts per serving (2 tablespoons [32 g/1.1 oz]):

Total carbs:	Fiber:	Net carbs:	Protein:	Fat:	Energy:	Calories from:
3.7 g	**2.4 g**	**1.3 g**	**1.4 g**	**21.8 g**	**207 kcal**	**Carbs (2%)** **Protein (3%)** **Fat (95%)**

Berry Nut Butter

Brighten the flavor of your fat bombs with this luscious and fruity Berry Nut Butter.

Ingredients

¾ cup (110 g/3.9 oz) blanched almonds

⅔ cup (90 g/3.2 oz) macadamia nuts

½ cup (125 g/4.4 oz) coconut butter

Few drops liquid stevia, to taste (optional)

½ cup (110 g/3.9 oz) coconut oil

¾ cup (60 g/2.1 oz) freeze-dried berry powder (raspberry, strawberry, blackberry, or blueberry) or equivalent weight of whole freeze-dried berries

Instructions

In a food processor, combine the almonds, macadamia nuts, and coconut butter. Add the stevia (if using), and process until smooth. The exact amount of time depends on your processor.

Add the coconut oil and berry powder or freeze-dried berries. Pulse again until combined. Spoon the butter into a glass container. Seal and store for 1 week at room temperature or refrigerate for up to 3 months. Note that the butter will become liquid at room temperature.

Tip

Create your own nut butter creations by replacing the berry powder with these alternatives: ¼ cup (25 g/0.9 oz) beetroot powder, 1 to 2 tablespoons (8 to 16 g/0.3 to 0.6 oz) pumpkin spice mix, 1 to 2 teaspoons turmeric, 1 tablespoon (5 g/0.2 oz) matcha powder, or 1 tablespoon (6 g/0.2 oz) lemon or orange zest.

Nutrition facts per serving (2 tablespoons [32 g/1.1 oz])

Total carbs:	Fiber:	Net carbs:	Protein:	Fat:	Energy:	Calories from:
6.4 g	**3.6 g**	**2.7 g**	**2.8 g**	**19.7 g**	**197 kcal**	**Carbs (5%)** **Protein (6%)** **Fat (89%)**

Yield:
About 1⅔ cups (405 g/ 14.3 oz)

Hands-on time:
10 mins

Overall time:
15 mins

Almond Bliss Butter

This treat will remind you of those fun-size candy bars you got in your Halloween goodie bag. If you adored those chocolate-coated, almond-studded delights, you'll feel like a kid again when you try this rich, delicious nut butter.

Ingredients

2 cups (150 g/5.3 oz) unsweetened shredded coconut

½ cup (75 g/2.6 oz) almonds

2.5 ounces (70 g) dark chocolate, 85 percent cacao solids or more

2.5 ounces (70 g) cacao butter

¼ cup (40 g/1.4 oz) erythritol or Swerve

Few drops liquid stevia, to taste (optional)

Instructions

Preheat the oven to 350°F (175°C, or gas mark 4). Spread the coconut and almonds on a baking sheet. Place it in the preheated oven and roast for 5 to 8 minutes, or until the coconut is lightly golden. Stir once or twice to prevent burning. Remove from the oven and set aside for a few minutes to cool.

In a food processor, combine the coconut, almonds, dark chocolate, cacao butter, and erythritol or Swerve. Pulse until smooth. The exact amount of time depends on your processor. Add the stevia (if using), and pulse again. Spoon the butter into a glass container. Seal and store at room temperature for up to 1 week, or refrigerate for up to 3 months.

Nutrition facts per serving (2 tablespoons [32 g/1.1 oz])

Total carbs:	Fiber:	Net carbs:	Protein:	Fat:	Energy:	Calories from:
5.9 g	**3.2 g**	**2.8 g**	**4.4 g**	**11.8 g**	**147 kcal**	**Carbs (8%)** **Protein (12%)** **Fat (80%)**

Spiced Maple and Pecan Butter

The combination of maple, pecan, and cinnamon smacks of a cool, crisp fall morning, and this sugar-free nut butter captures those rich, spicy flavors to enjoy any time.

Ingredients

3 cups (300 g/10.6 oz) pecans

1 to 2 teaspoons natural maple extract

½ teaspoon ground cinnamon

1 teaspoon sugar-free vanilla extract or ½ teaspoon vanilla powder

Pinch salt

Instructions

In a food processor, combine the pecans, maple extract, cinnamon, vanilla, and salt. Process until smooth. The exact amount of time depends on your processor. Spoon the butter into a glass container. Seal and store at room temperature for up to 1 week or refrigerate for up to 3 months.

Nutrition facts per serving (2 tablespoons [32 g/1.1 oz])

Total carbs:	Fiber:	Net carbs:	Protein:	Fat:	Energy:	Calories from:
4.6 g	**3.1 g**	**1.4 g**	**2.9 g**	**22.3 g**	**216 kcal**	**Carbs (3%)** **Protein (5%)** **Fat (92%)**

Yield:
**About 1¼
cups (310 g/
10.9 oz)**

Hands-on time:
5 mins

Overall time:
10 mins

Tips

✳ For healthy food extracts, use
unsweetened food extracts that are free
from propylene glycol and any added
sugar. Other common ingredients found
in food extracts include water, natural
oils, alcohol, and glycerin. You shouldn't
use alcohol if your primary aim is to
lose weight, but small amounts in food
extracts won't do any harm. Another
ingredient that turns up is glycerin,
which is a liquid by-product of making
soap. It belongs to a special category
of carbohydrates called *polyols*.
Glycerin has a minimal effect on
blood sugar levels and can be used
in small quantities.

✳ Certain food extracts can also be
swapped for a few drops of essential
oils, like orange, lemon, and mint.

Chocolate Chip Cookie Butter

There's no need to say good-bye to cookies—or chocolate—when you're eating low carb. This decadent butter is the proof, and it's one of my absolute favorites!

Ingredients

For the cookies:

1½ cups (150 g/5.3 oz) almond flour

⅓ cup (50 g/1.8 oz) erythritol or Swerve

½ teaspoon baking soda mixed with 1 teaspoon cream of tartar, or 1 teaspoon gluten-free baking powder

Pinch salt

1 teaspoon sugar-free vanilla extract or ½ teaspoon vanilla powder

1 teaspoon freshly grated lemon zest

2 large egg yolks

2 tablespoons (30 g/1.1 oz) butter, ghee, or coconut oil at room temperature

For the cookie butter:

Crushed cookies

½ cup (112 g/4 oz) unsalted butter or ghee or coconut oil, at room temperature

½ cup (90 g/3.2 oz) dark chocolate chips, 85 percent cacao solids or more, or make your own (see Homemade Dark Chocolate [page 32])

Few drops liquid stevia, to taste (optional)

Nutrition facts per serving (2 tablespoons [32 g/1.1 oz])

Total carbs:	Fiber:	Net carbs:	Protein:	Fat:	Energy:	Calories from:
3.9 g	**1.5 g**	**2.4 g**	**3.3 g**	**16.6 g**	**170 kcal**	**Carbs (6%)** **Protein (7%)** **Fat (87%)**

Yield:
About 1¾ cups (470 g/ 16.6 oz)

Hands-on time:
10 mins

Overall time:
30 mins

Tip
Instead of vanilla extract and lemon, try cinnamon or pumpkin spice mix and freshly grated orange zest.

Instructions
Preheat the oven to 300°F (150°C, or gas mark 2).

To make the cookies: In a mixing bowl, combine the almond flour, erythritol or Swerve, baking soda and cream of tartar, and salt. Mix well to combine. Add the vanilla, lemon zest, egg yolks, and butter or ghee. Mix together well with your hands.

Place the dough on a sheet of parchment paper. Top with another sheet of parchment and roll out to create a large cookie about ¼ inch thick. Transfer to a baking sheet and place it in the preheated oven. Bake for 12 to 15 minutes, or until lightly browned and crispy. Remove from the oven and cool to room temperature. When cool, break into smaller pieces.

To make the cookie butter: In a food processor, pulse together the cookie pieces and butter, ghee, or coconut oil until smooth. Add the chocolate chips. For a sweeter taste, add the stevia (if using). Pulse quickly to combine. Transfer to a sealed container and refrigerate for up to 1 week or use to make Cookie Dough Cups (page 75).

Yield:
About 1⅓ cups (330 g/ 11.6 oz)

Hands-on time:
5 mins

Overall time:
10–15 mins

Pistachio-Coconut Butter

Pistachio nuts are like potato chips—it's impossible to eat just one. Get your fix with this creamy nut butter that's packed with pistachios, macadamia nuts, and coconut.

Ingredients

For cookies:

1 cup (120 g/4.2 oz) pistachio nuts

1 cup (75 g/2.6 oz) shredded unsweetened coconut

1 cup (130 g/4.7 oz) macadamia nuts

1 teaspoon sugar-free vanilla extract or ½ teaspoon vanilla powder

Pinch salt

Instructions

In a food processor, combine the pistachios, coconut, macadamia nuts, vanilla, and salt. Pulse until smooth. The exact amount of time depends on your processor. Spoon the butter into a glass container. Seal and store at room temperature for up to 1 week or refrigerate for up to 3 months.

Tip

Intensify the flavor of this butter by using toasted pistachios nuts, macadamia nuts, and coconut. Preheat the oven to 350°F (175°C, or gas mark 4). Spread the pistachios, macadamia nuts, and coconut on a baking sheet. Place it in the preheated oven and toast for 5 to 8 minutes, or until the coconut is lightly golden. Stir once or twice to prevent burning. The pistachios will turn light brown, instead of green, and the flavor will be more intense.

Nutrition facts per serving (2 tablespoons [32 g/1.1 oz])

Total carbs:	Fiber:	Net carbs:	Protein:	Fat:	Energy:	Calories from:
6.7 g	**3.5 g**	**3.2 g**	**4.8 g**	**15.8 g**	**182 kcal**	**Carbs (7%)** **Protein (11%)** **Fat (82%)**

Pumpkin Sun Butter

Can't eat nuts? Never fear: you can still make fat bombs with this spiced, nut-free seed butter.

Ingredients

1½ cups (210 g/7.4 oz) sunflower seeds

½ cup (65 g/2.3 oz) pumpkin seeds

2 teaspoons ground cinnamon

Pinch salt

Instructions

In a food processor, combine the sunflower seeds, pumpkin seeds, cinnamon, and salt. Pulse until smooth. The exact amount of time depends on your processor. Spoon the butter into a glass container. Seal and store at room temperature for up to 1 week, or refrigerate for up to 3 months.

Nutrition facts per serving (2 tablespoons [32 g/1.1 oz])

Total carbs:	Fiber:	Net carbs:	Protein:	Fat:	Energy:	Calories from:
6.1 g	**2.8 g**	**3.3 g**	**7.3 g**	**16 g**	**183 kcal**	**Carbs (7%)** **Protein (16%)** **Fat (77%)**

Hands-on time:
10 mins

Overall time:
**15 minutes
+ chilling time**

Homemade Dark Chocolate Three Ways

This essential recipe shows you how to make healthy, sugar-free chocolate in just a few simple steps.

Yield:
225 g/8 oz

Yield:
213 g/7.5 oz

Yield:
195 g/6.8 oz

Dark Chocolate Using Unsweetened Chocolate

Ingredients

3 ounces (85 g) unsweetened chocolate

3 ounces (85 g) cacao butter

⅓ cup (50 g/1.8 oz) powdered erythritol or Swerve

1 teaspoon sugar-free vanilla extract or ½ teaspoon vanilla powder

Pinch salt

Few drops liquid stevia, to taste (optional)

Instructions

Melt the unsweetened chocolate and cacao butter in a double boiler, or heat-proof bowl placed over a small saucepan filled with 1 cup (235 ml/8 oz) of water, over medium heat. Remove from the heat and set aside. Stir in the erythritol or Swerve, vanilla, and salt. If you want a sweeter taste, add the stevia. Pour the chocolate into candy or chocolate molds or onto a parchment-lined baking sheet. Let it harden at room temperature, or in the refrigerator. Remove from the molds. Store at room temperature or refrigerate for up to 3 months.

Nutrition facts per serving (28 g/1 oz)

Total carbs: **3 g**
Fiber: **1.5 g**
Net carbs: **1.5 g**
Protein: **1.5 g**
Fat: **16.2 g**
Energy: **164 kcal**
Calories from: **Carbs (4%), Protein (4%), Fat (92%)**

Dark Chocolate Using Cacao Powder

Ingredients

4 ounces (112 g) cacao butter

½ cup (40 g/1.4 oz) unsweetened cacao powder

⅓ cup (50 g/1.8 oz) powdered erythritol or Swerve

1 teaspoon sugar-free vanilla extract or ½ teaspoon vanilla powder

Pinch salt

Few drops liquid stevia, to taste (optional)

Instructions

Melt the cacao butter in a double boiler, or heat-proof bowl placed over a small saucepan filled with 1 cup (235 ml/8 oz) of water, over medium heat. Remove from the heat and set aside. Stir in the cacao powder, erythritol or Swerve, vanilla, and salt. If you want a sweeter taste, add the stevia. Pour into candy or chocolate molds and harden at room temperature or in the refrigerator. Once hardened, remove from the molds and keep in an airtight container. Store at room temperature or refrigerate for up to 3 months.

Nutrition facts per serving (28 g/1 oz)

Total carbs: **3.5 g**
Fiber: **1.8 g**
Net carbs: **1.7 g**
Protein: **1.1 g**
Fat: **15.9 g**
Energy: **150 kcal**
Calories from: **Carbs (4%), Protein (3%), Fat (93%)**

Dark Chocolate Using Coconut Oil

Ingredients

½ cup (110 g/3.9 oz) coconut oil

½ cup (40 g/1.5 oz) unsweetened cacao powder

¼ cup (40 g/1.4 oz) powdered erythritol or Swerve

1 teaspoon sugar-free vanilla extract or ½ teaspoon vanilla powder

Pinch salt

Few drops liquid stevia, to taste (optional)

Instructions

Melt the coconut oil in a double boiler, or heat-proof bowl placed over a small saucepan filled with 1 cup (235 ml/8 oz) of water, over medium heat. Once melted, add the cacao powder, erythritol or Swerve, vanilla, and salt. If you want a sweeter taste, add the stevia. Pour into candy or chocolate molds and harden in the refrigerator. Once hardened, remove from the molds and store in an airtight container. Always store in the refrigerator: coconut oil melts at room temperature. Refrigerate for up to 3 months or freeze for up to 6 months.

Nutrition facts per serving (28 g/1 oz)

Total carbs: **3.7 g**
Fiber: **1.9 g**
Net carbs: **1.8 g**
Protein: **1.1 g**
Fat: **16.4 g**
Energy: **151 kcal**
Calories from: **Carbs (4%), Protein (3%), Fat (93%)**

Homemade White Chocolate

Packed with healthy fats and made from real food ingredients (no additives here!), my Homemade White Chocolate is sugar-free and infused with fragrant vanilla.

Ingredients

6 ounces (170 g) cacao butter

1 cup (120 g/4.2 oz) coconut milk powder

⅓ cup (50 g/1.8 oz) powdered erythritol or Swerve

2 teaspoons sugar-free vanilla extract or 1 teaspoon vanilla powder

Pinch salt

Few drops liquid stevia, to taste (optional)

Instructions

Melt the cacao butter in a double boiler, or heat-proof bowl placed over a small saucepan filled with 1 cup (235 ml/8 oz) of water, over medium heat. Remove from the heat and set aside. Add the coconut milk powder, erythritol or Swerve, vanilla, and salt. If you want a sweeter taste, add the stevia. Pour the mixture into a food processor. Pulse for 30 to 60 seconds, or until smooth. Pour into candy or chocolate molds and let the chocolate harden in the refrigerator. Once solid, remove from the molds. Store at room temperature or refrigerate for up to 3 months.

Nutrition facts per serving (28 g/1 oz)

Total carbs:	Fiber:	Net carbs:	Protein:	Fat:	Energy:	Calories from:
2.7 g	**0.1 g**	**2.6 g**	**0.7 g**	**19.8 g**	**191 kcal**	**Carbs (5%)** **Protein (2%)** **Fat (93%)**

Yield:
About 12 ounces (340 g)

Hands-on time:
10 mins

Overall time:
15 mins + chilling time

Tips

✱ For an extra nutritional boost, swap ½ cup (60 g/2.1 oz) of coconut milk powder with ½ cup (40 g/1.4 oz) of lucuma powder.

✱ What is lucuma powder? Lucuma, a subtropical fruit, is an anti-inflammatory superfood also known as "Gold of the Incas." It is high in carotene, iron, vitamin B_3, and fiber and has a light orange color. The powder made from this fruit adds natural sweetness to the chocolate, and makes it creamier. Keep in mind that lucuma powder has more than twice as many carbs as coconut milk powder, so stick to the suggested amounts. Using lucuma powder in this recipe will result in 4.3 grams of net carbs per serving.

Chapter 3

Sweet Fat Bombs

Finding healthy, low-carb treats can feel like a bit of a challenge sometimes. That's why this chapter is packed with recipes for easy-to-make sweet snacks like truffles, candies, chocolate bark, fudge, and more. They're all delicious ways to sneak healthy fats into your diet—minus the sweeteners and additives found in most store-bought snack options, of course. And they're proof that a sugar-free, keto-friendly diet is anything but boring!

Yield:
15 fat bombs

Hands-on time:
15 mins

Overall time:
10 mins + chilling time

Almond and Cashew Chocolate Candies

Put your stash of nut and seed butters to good use with these chocolatey, easy-to-make treats.

Ingredients

1 recipe (195 g/6.8 oz) Homemade Dark Chocolate made with coconut oil (page 33)

¼ cup (65 g/2.3 oz) Almond and Cashew Butter (page 16)

Instructions

Spoon 2 teaspoons of the dark chocolate into a silicone candy mold or mini muffin cups. Each mold or mini muffin cup should hold over a tablespoon, so it will be about half full. Refrigerate for a few minutes until the chocolate solidifies.

When solidified, add ½ teaspoon of the Almond and Cashew Butter to each mold. Top each with another 1 teaspoon of the remaining chocolate and refrigerate again for 30 minutes to 1 hour, or until firm. Keep refrigerated for up to 1 week or freeze for up to 3 months. Note that coconut oil and coconut butter soften at room temperature.

Tip

Coconut oil is high in medium-chain triglycerides (MCTs), saturated fats our body can digest very easily. MCTs behave differently than other fats when ingested, and are passed directly to the liver for use as an immediate form of energy. Athletes commonly use MCTs to improve and enhance performance and support fat loss.

Nutrition facts per serving (1 fat bomb)

Total carbs:	Fiber:	Net carbs:	Protein:	Fat:	Energy:	Calories from:
2.5 g	**1.1 g**	**1.3 g**	**1.2 g**	**10.2 g**	**98 kcal**	**Carbs (5%)** **Protein (5%)** **Fat (90%)**

Yield:
10 fat bombs

Hands-on time:
20 mins

Overall time:
**20 mins +
chilling time**

Coconut Candies

Sweets don't have to be high in carbs. These versatile candies can be made with your favorite flavors—and, happily, they won't spike your blood sugar.

Ingredients

For the candies:

½ cup (125 g/4.4 oz) coconut butter, at room temperature

½ cup (110 g/3.9 oz) coconut oil, at room temperature

¼ cup (40 g/1.4 oz) powdered erythritol or Swerve

1 teaspoon sugar-free extract of your choice (such as vanilla, lemon, peppermint, or almond)

Few drops liquid stevia, to taste (optional)

For the coating (or use any Homemade Dark Chocolate recipe [page 33]):

3 ounces (85 g) extra-dark 90 percent chocolate

1.2 ounces (35 g) cacao butter

Instructions

To make the candies: In a bowl, combine the coconut butter, coconut oil, erythritol or Swerve, and flavoring extract. Mix until well combined. If you want a sweeter taste, add the stevia.

Fill a silicone candy mold, silicone ice-cube trays, or mini muffin cups with about 1-tablespoon (15 g/0.5 oz) portions of the coconut mixture. Freeze for 30 minutes to 1 hour.

To make the coating: Melt the dark chocolate and cacao butter in a double boiler, or heat-proof bowl placed over a small saucepan filled with 1 cup (235 ml/8 oz) of water, over medium heat. Mix well. Let the chocolate cool before use. It shouldn't be hot but should still be liquid. If you are using any of the Homemade Dark Chocolate recipes (page 33), you may need as much as 5.3 to 5.6 ounces (150 to 160 g) to coat all the fat bombs.

Gently pierce each frozen candy with a toothpick or a fork. Working one at a time, hold each candy over the melted chocolate and spoon the chocolate over it to coat completely. Turn the stick as you work until the coating is solidified. Place the candies on a parchment-lined tray and drizzle any remaining chocolate over them.

Refrigerate the coated candies for at least 15 minutes to harden. Keep refrigerated for up to 1 month or freeze for up to 3 months.

Nutrition facts per serving (1 fat bomb)

Total carbs:	Fiber:	Net carbs:	Protein:	Fat:	Energy:	Calories from:
2.3 g	**1.2 g**	**1 g**	**0.8 g**	**13.1 g**	**123 kcal**	**Carbs (3%)** **Protein (3%)** **Fat (94%)**

Easy Lemon Fat Bombs

These simple, citrusy fat bombs take just a few minutes to make. For a Key lime pie-inspired twist, use organic lime zest in place of the lemon zest.

Ingredients

7.1 ounces (200 g) coconut butter

¼ cup (55 g/1.9 oz) coconut oil

1 tablespoon (6 g/0.2 oz) freshly grated lemon zest or 1 teaspoon sugar-free lemon extract

2 tablespoons (20 g/0.7 oz) powdered erythritol or Swerve

Few drops liquid stevia, to taste (optional)

Instructions

Melt the coconut butter and coconut oil in a double boiler, or heat-proof bowl placed over a small saucepan filled with 1 cup (235 ml/8 oz) of water, over medium heat. Add the lemon zest or extract and erythritol or Swerve. If you want a sweeter taste, add the stevia. Mix well to combine.

Fill a silicone candy mold or mini muffin cups with about 1-tablespoon (15 g/0.5 oz) portions of the coconut mixture and place them on a tray. Refrigerate for 30 minutes to 1 hour, or until solid.

Keep refrigerated for up to 1 month or freeze for up to 3 months. Note that coconut oil and coconut butter soften at room temperature.

Nutrition facts per serving (1 fat bomb)

Total carbs:	Fiber:	Net carbs:	Protein:	Fat:	Energy:	Calories from:
2.6 g	**1.8 g**	**0.8 g**	**0.8 g**	**11.9 g**	**112 kcal**	**Carbs (3%)** **Protein (3%)** **Fat (94%)**

Yield:
16 fat bombs

Hands-on time:
10 mins

Overall time:
10 mins + chilling time

Quick Orange Fat Bombs

If you liked those orange-and-cream ice pops as a kid, you'll love these refreshing, high-fat treats. Keep a batch on hand so you can grab one for a quick snack attack.

Ingredients

7.1 ounces (200 g) coconut butter

¼ cup (55 g/1.9 oz) coconut oil

1 tablespoon (6 g/0.2 oz) freshly grated orange zest or 1 teaspoon sugar-free orange extract

2 tablespoons (20 g/0.7 oz) powdered erythritol or Swerve

Few drops liquid stevia, to taste (optional)

2 heaping tablespoons (28 g/1 oz) cacao nibs or dark chocolate chips

Instructions

Melt the coconut butter and coconut oil in a double boiler, or heat-proof bowl placed over a small saucepan filled with 1 cup (235 ml/8 oz) of water, over medium heat. Add the orange zest or extract and erythritol or Swerve. If you want a sweeter taste, add the stevia. Mix well to combine.

Fill a silicone candy mold or mini muffin cups with about 1-tablespoon (15 g/10.5 oz) portions of the coconut-orange mixture. Top with the cacao nibs or chocolate chips and place them on a tray. Refrigerate for 30 minutes to 1 hour, or until solid.

Keep refrigerated for up to 1 week or freeze for up to 3 months. Note that coconut oil and coconut butter soften at room temperature.

Nutrition facts per serving (1 fat bomb)

Total carbs:	Fiber:	Net carbs:	Protein:	Fat:	Energy:	Calories from:
3.2 g	**2 g**	**1.2 g**	**1 g**	**12.8 g**	**123 kcal**	**Carbs (4%)** **Protein (3%)** **Fat (93%)**

Vanilla Fat Bombs

Coconut oil and macadamia nuts are some of the healthiest foods on the planet, so you'll get a double dose of goodness with these delicious Vanilla Fat Bombs.

Ingredients

1 cup (130 g/4.6 oz) macadamia nuts

¼ cup (55 g/1.9 oz) coconut oil, at room temperature

¼ cup (56 g/2 oz) unsalted butter, ghee, or more coconut oil, at room temperature

2 teaspoons sugar-free vanilla extract or 1 teaspoon vanilla powder

2 tablespoons (20 g/0.7 oz) powdered erythritol or Swerve

Few drops liquid stevia, to taste (optional)

Instructions

In a blender, pulse the macadamia nuts until smooth. Add the coconut oil, butter or ghee, vanilla, erythritol or Swerve, and stevia (if using) and pulse again to combine.

Fill a silicone candy mold, silicone ice-cube tray, or mini muffin cups with 1½-tablespoon (20 g/0.7 oz) portions of the mixture. Refrigerate for at least 30 minutes, or until solid.

Pop the fat bombs out of the molds and keep refrigerated for up to 1 week (coconut oil and butter soften at room temperature) or freeze for up to 3 months.

Nutrition facts per serving (1 fat bomb)

Total carbs:	Fiber:	Net carbs:	Protein:	Fat:	Energy:	Calories from:
1.6 g	**1 g**	**0.6 g**	**0.8 g**	**14.4 g**	**132 kcal**	**Carbs (2%)** **Protein (2%)** **Fat (96%)**

Yield:
14 fat bombs

Hands-on time:
10 mins

Overall time:
10 mins + chilling time

Tip
To powder the erythritol, place it in a clean blender or coffee grinder and pulse until fine. I always keep 1 to 2 cups of powdered erythritol on hand in my pantry, in a sealed jar to avoid clumping.

Eggnog Truffles

Coated in coconut butter, these eggnog-flavored truffles are bite-size celebrations—perfect for the holiday season.

Yield:
9 truffles

Hands-on time:
20 mins

Overall time:
20 mins + chilling time

Ingredients

For the truffles:

½ cup (about 125 g/4.4 oz) Eggnog-Macadamia Butter (page 22)

2 tablespoons (28 g/1 oz) coconut oil

⅓ cup (40 g/1.4 oz) coconut flour

⅓ cup (25 g/0.9 oz) unsweetened shredded coconut

1 tablespoon (10 g/0.4 oz) powdered erythritol or Swerve

¼ teaspoon ground nutmeg

¼ teaspoon ground cinnamon

Few drops liquid stevia, to taste (optional)

1 tablespoon (14 g/0.5 oz) macadamia oil or other light-tasting oil, for shaping the truffles

For the coating:

¼ cup (56 g/2 oz) coconut butter, melted

2 tablespoons (28 g/1 oz) coconut oil, melted

Pinch nutmeg

Instructions

To make the truffles: In a mixing bowl, mix together the macadamia butter, coconut oil, coconut flour, coconut, erythritol or Swerve, nutmeg, and cinnamon until well combined. If you want a sweeter taste, add a few drops of stevia. Refrigerate the dough for 30 minutes to 1 hour, or until solid enough to form truffles.

To shape the truffles, dip a spoon or a melon baller in warm water and scoop out 9 balls of the chilled dough. Lightly coat your hands in macadamia oil. Roll the truffles between your palms to form spheres about twice the size of standard truffles. Place them on a parchment-lined tray and freeze for about 30 minutes.

To make the coating: In a small saucepan, melt the coconut butter and coconut oil over low heat. Add the nutmeg. Mix well to combine and set aside.

Gently pierce each frozen truffle with a toothpick or a fork. Working one at a time, hold each truffle over the melted coconut butter and spoon the coating over it to coat completely. Turn the stick as you work until the coating is solidified. Place the coated truffles on a parchment-lined tray and drizzle any remaining coating over them.

Refrigerate the coated truffles for at least 15 minutes to harden. Keep refrigerated for up to 1 month or freeze for up to 3 months.

Nutrition facts per serving (1 truffle):

Total carbs:	Fiber:	Net carbs:	Protein:	Fat:	Energy:	Calories from:
5.5 g	**3.5 g**	**1.9 g**	**2.7 g**	**21.6 g**	**218 kcal**	**Carbs (4%)** **Protein (5%)** **Fat (91%)**

Yield:
10 truffles

Hands-on time:
15 mins

Overall time:
15 mins + chilling time

Chocolate-Avocado Truffles

Avocado doesn't turn up in desserts as often as it should, since it's high in healthy fats and potassium—and its neutral taste and creamy texture make it a handy tool for creating decadent, low-carb chocolate truffles!

Ingredients

For the truffles:

3.5 ounces (100 g) dark chocolate, 90 percent cacao solids or more, or use any of the Homemade Dark Chocolate recipes (page 32)

1 medium (150 g/5.3 oz) avocado, peeled and pitted

¼ cup (60 g/2.1 oz) coconut butter

1 teaspoon sugar-free vanilla extract or ½ teaspoon vanilla powder

½ teaspoon ground cinnamon

Pinch salt

Few drops liquid stevia, to taste (optional)

1 tablespoon (14 g/0.5 oz) macadamia oil or avocado oil, or other light-tasting oil, for shaping the truffles

For the coating:

2 tablespoons (10 g/0.4 oz) unsweetened cacao powder, or enough toasted almond flakes, shredded unsweetened coconut, or coconut flakes to cover.

Instructions

To make the truffles: Melt the dark chocolate in a double boiler, or heat-proof bowl placed over a small saucepan filled with 1 cup (235 ml/8 oz) of water, over medium heat. Remove from the heat and set aside.

In a food processor, combine the avocado, coconut butter, vanilla, cinnamon, and salt. Pulse until smooth. With the processor running, slowly drizzle in the melted chocolate. Mix until well combined with the avocado. If you want a sweeter taste, add the stevia. Transfer the mixture to a bowl and refrigerate for about 1 hour, or until solid.

To shape the truffles, dip a spoon or a melon baller in warm water and scoop out 10 balls of the chilled mixture. Lightly coat your hands in macadamia oil. Roll the truffles between your palms to form spheres about twice the size of standard truffles. Coat them immediately after shaping.

To make the coating: Roll the truffles in your favorite coating. Refrigerate the coated truffles for at least 15 minutes to harden. Keep refrigerated for up to 1 week or freeze for up to 3 months.

Total carbs:	Fiber:	Net carbs:	Protein:	Fat:	Energy:	Calories from:
5.3 g	**3 g**	**2.3 g**	**1.9 g**	**12.7 g**	**129 kcal**	**Carbs (7%)** **Protein (6%)** **Fat (87%)**

Red Velvet Truffles

There's no need to rely on artificial food coloring to make these beautiful truffles. Instead, use beetroot powder to give them a vivid, deep red tint.

Ingredients

For the truffles:

½ cup (125 g/4.4 oz) coconut butter

¼ cup (55 g/1.9 oz) coconut oil

½ cup (60 g/2.1 oz) coconut flour

¼ cup (40 g/1.4 oz) powdered erythritol or Swerve

2 teaspoons sugar-free vanilla extract or 1 teaspoon vanilla powder, or use the same amount of any food extract: cherry and raspberry work well

2 tablespoons (12 g/0.4 oz) beetroot powder

Pinch salt

Few drops liquid stevia, to taste (optional)

1 tablespoon (14 g/0.5 oz) macadamia oil, or other light tasting oil, for shaping the truffles

For the coating:

3.5 ounces (100 g) Homemade White Chocolate (page 34)

Instructions

To make the truffles: Melt the coconut butter and coconut oil in a double boiler, or heat-proof bowl placed over a small saucepan filled with 1 cup (235 ml/8 oz) of water, over medium heat. Remove from the heat and set aside. Stir in the coconut flour, erythritol or Swerve, vanilla or other extract, beetroot powder, and salt. If you want a sweeter taste, add the stevia and mix again. Refrigerate the mixture for about 30 minutes, or until just firm enough to form truffles.

To shape the truffles, dip a spoon or a melon baller in warm water and scoop out 10 balls of the chilled mixture. Lightly coat your hands in macadamia oil. Roll the truffles between your palms to form spheres about twice the size of standard truffles. Place the truffles on a parchment-lined tray. Freeze for about 30 minutes.

To make the coating: Melt the white chocolate in a double boiler, or heat-proof bowl placed over a small saucepan filled with 1 cup (235 ml/8 oz) of water, over medium heat. Remove from the heat and set aside to cool. The chocolate should not be hot when you use it for coating.

Nutrition facts per serving (1 truffle)

Total carbs:	Fiber:	Net carbs:	Protein:	Fat:	Energy:	Calories from:
6.5 g	**3.2 g**	**3.3 g**	**2.2 g**	**21.7 g**	**225 kcal**	**Carbs (6%)** **Protein (4%)** **Fat (90%)**

Yield:
10 truffles

Hands-on time:
20 mins

Overall time:
**20 mins +
chilling time**

Gently pierce each frozen truffle with a toothpick or a fork. Working one at a time, hold each truffle over the melted white chocolate and spoon the chocolate over it to coat completely. Turn the stick as you work until the coating is solidified. Place the coated truffles on a parchment-lined tray and drizzle any remaining coating over them.

Refrigerate the coated truffles for at least 15 minutes to harden. Keep refrigerated for up to 1 month or freeze for up to 3 months.

Chocolate-Hazelnut Truffles

My Chocolate-Hazelnut Butter is a low-carb take on the sugar-laden store-bought variety. Use it to whip up these fudgy, hazelnut-crusted truffles!

Ingredients

For the truffles:

½ recipe (1 cup/250 g/8.8 oz) Chocolate-Hazelnut Butter (page 20)

⅓ cup (73 g/2.6 oz) coconut oil

¼ cup (20 g/0.7 oz) cacao powder

2 tablespoons (20 g/0.7 oz) powdered erythritol or Swerve

Few drops liquid stevia, to taste (optional)

1 tablespoon (14 g/0.5 oz) macadamia oil or other light-tasting oil, for shaping the truffles

For the coating:

½ cup (75 g/2 oz) crushed hazelnuts, raw or toasted

Instructions

To make the truffles: Melt the nut butter and coconut oil in a double boiler, or heat-proof bowl placed over a small saucepan filled with 1 cup (235 ml/8 oz) of water, over medium heat. Remove from the heat and set aside.

Add the cacao powder and erythritol or Swerve. Mix until well combined. If you want a sweeter taste, add the stevia. Refrigerate the mixture for 30 minutes to 1 hour, or until firm enough to form truffles.

To shape the truffles, dip a spoon or melon baller in warm water and scoop out 10 balls of the chilled mixture. Lightly coat your hands in macadamia oil. Roll the truffles between your palms to form spheres about twice the size of standard truffles. Coat them immediately after shaping.

To make the coating: Roll the truffles in the crushed hazelnuts. Refrigerate the coated truffles for at least 15 minutes to harden. Keep refrigerated for up to 1 week or freeze for up to 3 months.

Nutrition facts per serving (1 truffle)

Total carbs:	Fiber:	Net carbs:	Protein:	Fat:	Energy:	Calories from:
6 g	**3.1 g**	**2.9 g**	**3.8 g**	**23.4 g**	**231 kcal**	**Carbs (5%)** **Protein (6%)** **Fat (89%)**

Yield:	Hands-on time:	Overall time:
14 truffles	**15 mins**	**15 mins + chilling time**

Amaretto Truffles

The rich, lush flavor of almonds takes center stage in these nutty, sugar-free truffles. Roll them in toasted almonds for some extra crunch.

Ingredients

For the truffles:

½ cup (125 g/4.4 oz) almond butter or Almond and Cashew Butter (page 16)

¼ cup (55 g/1.9 oz) coconut oil

½ cup (112 g/4 oz) unsalted butter, ghee, or coconut oil, at room temperature

¼ cup (40 g/1.4 oz) powdered erythritol or Swerve

1 to 2 teaspoons sugar-free almond extract

Few drops liquid stevia, to taste (optional)

1 tablespoon (14 g/0.5 oz) macadamia oil or other light-tasting oil, for shaping the truffles

For the coating:

3 ounces (85 g) flaked almonds

Instructions

To make the truffles: Melt the nut butter and coconut oil in a double boiler, or heat-proof bowl placed over a small saucepan filled with 1 cup (235 ml/8 oz) of water, over medium heat. Remove from the heat and set aside.

Stir in the butter, ghee, or coconut oil, erythritol or Swerve, and almond extract, mixing well to combine. If you want a sweeter taste, add the stevia. Refrigerate for 30 minutes to 1 hour, or until firm enough to form truffles.

To shape the truffles, dip a spoon or melon baller in warm water and scoop out 14 balls of the chilled mixture. Lightly coat your hands in macadamia oil. Roll the truffles between your palms to form spheres about twice the size of standard truffles. Coat them immediately after shaping.

To make the coating: Place the almond flakes in a dry, hot skillet and toast for a few minutes, until fragrant. Stir frequently to prevent burning. Transfer to a bowl to cool completely.

Roll the truffles in the flaked almonds. Refrigerate the coated truffles for at least 15 minutes to harden. Keep refrigerated for up to 1 week or freeze for up to 3 months.

Nutrition facts per serving (1 truffle)

Total carbs:	Fiber:	Net carbs:	Protein:	Fat:	Energy:	Calories from:
3.5 g	**2.1 g**	**1.3 g**	**3.9 g**	**20.7 g**	**214 kcal**	**Carbs (2%)** **Protein (8%)** **Fat (90%)**

Dark Chocolate and Orange Truffles

I love the classic combination of orange and dark chocolate: it's intense, beguiling, and completely addictive—and so are these super-filling fat bombs.

Ingredients

For the truffles:

1 can (400 ml/13.5 fl oz) coconut milk or equivalent amount of heavy whipping cream

¼ cup plus 1 tablespoon (50 g/1.8 oz) powdered erythritol or Swerve

1 tablespoon (6 g/0.2 oz) freshly grated orange zest

6 ounces (170 g) unsweetened chocolate

¼ cup (56 g/2 oz) unsalted butter or coconut oil, at room temperature

Pinch salt

Few drops liquid stevia, to taste (optional)

1 tablespoon (14 g/0.5 oz) macadamia oil or other light-tasting oil, for shaping the truffles

For the coating (or use any Homemade Dark Chocolate recipe [page 32]):

2.5 ounces (70 g) extra-dark 90 percent chocolate, broken into small pieces

1 ounce (28 g) cacao butter

Freshly grated orange zest, for garnish

Instructions

To make the truffles: In a small saucepan set over medium heat, bring the coconut milk or cream to a boil. Reduce the heat to low. Add the erythritol or Swerve, stirring until dissolved. Cook, stirring occasionally, for 20 to 30 minutes, or until the milk is creamy and reduced by about half. Remove from the heat, stir in the orange zest, and set aside to cool for a few minutes.

In a mixing bowl, place the unsweetened chocolate. Slowly pour the coconut milk mixture over it and stir until the chocolate is completely melted and smooth. Add the butter or coconut oil and mix until well combined. If the chocolate mixture separates, add a splash of boiling water or place in a blender and process until smooth. Add the salt. If you want a sweeter taste, add the stevia. Cool and then refrigerate for 1 hour, or until firm.

To shape the truffles, dip a spoon or melon baller in warm water and scoop out 12 balls of the chilled mixture. Lightly coat your hands in macadamia oil. Roll the truffles between your palms to form spheres about twice the size of standard truffles. Place them on a parchment-lined tray and freeze for about 30 minutes.

Nutrition facts per serving (1 truffle)

Total carbs:	Fiber:	Net carbs:	Protein:	Fat:	Energy:	Calories from:
6.2 g	**2.8 g**	**3.3 g**	**3.3 g**	**24 g**	**245 kcal**	**Carbs (6%)** **Protein (5%)** **Fat (89%)**

Yield:
12 truffles

Hands-on time:
20 mins

Overall time:
**40 mins +
chilling time**

To make the coating: Melt the dark chocolate and cacao butter in a double boiler, or heat-proof bowl placed over a small saucepan filled with 1 cup (235 ml/ 8 oz) of water, over medium heat. Remove from the heat and set aside to cool. If you are using any of the Homemade Dark Chocolate recipes, you may need as much as 4.6 to 4.9 ounces (130 to 140 g) to coat all the fat bombs.

Gently pierce each frozen truffle with a toothpick or a fork. Working one at a time, hold the truffle over the melted chocolate and spoon the chocolate over it to coat completely. Turn the stick as you work until the coating is solidified. Place the coated truffles on a parchment-lined tray and drizzle any remaining coating over them. Before they become completely solid, sprinkle with the orange zest. Refrigerate the coated truffles for at least 15 minutes to harden. Keep refrigerated for up to 1 week or freeze for up to 3 months.

Earl Grey Truffles

Earl Grey tea adds a delicate flavor to these dark chocolate truffles. Be sure to use high-quality tea: it really does yield a better result.

Ingredients

For the truffles:

⅔ cup (150 ml/5 fl oz) coconut milk or heavy whipping cream

½ cup (80 g/2.8 oz) powdered erythritol or Swerve

¼ cup (56 g/2 oz) unsalted butter, ghee, or coconut oil, at room temperature

1 tablespoon (5 g/0.2 oz) good-quality Earl Grey tea leaves

6 ounces (170 g) unsweetened chocolate, broken into small pieces

Pinch salt

Few drops liquid stevia, to taste (optional)

1 tablespoon (14 g/0.5 oz) macadamia oil or other light-tasting oil, for shaping the truffles

For the coating:

4.2 ounces (120 g) Homemade White Chocolate (page 34)

2 heaping tablespoons (28 g/1 oz) cacao nibs

Instructions

To make the truffles: In a saucepan, combine the coconut milk or cream, erythritol or Swerve, and butter, ghee, or oil. Bring to a boil. Immediately remove the mixture from the heat and stir in the tea. Cover and let it sit for 5 to 10 minutes.

In a bowl, place the unsweetened chocolate piece. Through a sieve, slowly pour the hot coconut milk over the chocolate, pressing on the tea leaves as the sieve catches them. Discard the tea leaves. Stir until the chocolate is completely melted and smooth. If the chocolate mixture separates, add a splash of boiling water or place in a blender and process until smooth. Add the salt. If you want a sweeter taste, add the stevia. Cool and refrigerate for 1 hour, or until firm.

To shape the truffles, dip a spoon or melon baller in warm water and scoop out 14 balls of the chilled mixture. Lightly coat your hands in macadamia oil. Roll the truffles between your palms to form spheres about twice the size of standard truffles. Place on a parchment-lined tray and freeze for about 30 minutes.

Nutrition facts per serving (1 truffle)

Total carbs:	Fiber:	Net carbs:	Protein:	Fat:	Energy:	Calories from:
5.1 g	**2 g**	**3.1 g**	**2.5 g**	**20.1 g**	**208 kcal**	**Carbs (6%)** **Protein (5%)** **Fat (89%)**

Yield:
14 truffles

Hands-on time:
20 mins

Overall time:
**20 mins +
chilling time**

To make the coating: Melt the white chocolate in a double boiler, or heat-proof bowl placed over a small saucepan filled with 1 cup (235 ml/8 oz) of water, over medium heat. Once melted, remove from the heat and set aside to cool.

Gently pierce each frozen truffle with a toothpick or a fork. Working one at a time, hold each truffle over the melted white chocolate and spoon the chocolate over it to coat completely. Turn the stick as you work until the coating is solidified. Place the coated truffles on a parchment-lined tray and drizzle any remaining coating over them. Before the truffles become completely solid, sprinkle them with the cacao nibs.

Refrigerate the coated truffles for at least 15 minutes to harden. Keep refrigerated for up to 1 week or freeze for up to 3 months.

Yield:
10 truffles

Hands-on time:
15 mins

Overall time:
**15 mins +
chilling time**

Coconut and Cinnamon Truffles

Cinnamon-spiced and full of heart-healthy nuts, these truffles are even better when they're rolled in toasted coconut.

Ingredients

For the truffles:

¾ cup (110 g/3.9 oz) almonds

¼ cup (30 g/1.1 oz) pecans

¼ cup (30 g/1.1 oz) Brazil nuts

2 tablespoons (28 g/1 oz) coconut oil

2 teaspoons ground cinnamon

1 teaspoon sugar-free vanilla extract or ½ teaspoon vanilla powder

¼ cup (40 g/1.4 oz) powdered erythritol or Swerve

Pinch salt

Few drops liquid stevia, to taste (optional)

1 tablespoon (14 g/0.5 oz) macadamia oil or other light-tasting oil, for shaping the truffles

For the coating:

⅓ cup (25 g/0.9 oz) unsweetened shredded coconut

Instructions

To make the truffles: In a food processor, combine the almonds, pecans, Brazil nuts, coconut oil, cinnamon, vanilla, erythritol or Swerve, and salt. Pulse until smooth. If you want a sweeter taste, add the stevia. Transfer to a bowl and refrigerate for 30 minutes to 1 hour, or until firm enough to form truffles.

If you prefer raw coconut, skip this next step. Preheat the oven to 350°F (175°C, or gas mark 4). Spread the shredded coconut on a baking sheet. Place it in the preheated oven and toast for 5 to 8 minutes, or until lightly golden. Stir once or twice to prevent burning. Remove from the oven and set aside.

To shape the truffles, dip a spoon or melon baller in warm water and scoop out 10 balls of the chilled mixture. Lightly coat your hands in macadamia oil. Roll the truffles between your palms to form spheres about twice the size of standard truffles. Coat them immediately after shaping.

To make the coating: Roll the truffles in the shredded coconut. Refrigerate the coated truffles for at least 15 minutes to harden. Keep refrigerated for up to 1 week or freeze for up to 3 months.

Nutrition facts per serving (1 truffle)

Total carbs:	Fiber:	Net carbs:	Protein:	Fat:	Energy:	Calories from:
4.4 g	**2.5 g**	**1.9 g**	**3.6 g**	**16.7 g**	**174 kcal**	**Carbs (5%)** **Protein (8%)** **Fat (87%)**

Pumpkin-Snickerdoodle Truffles

Indulge your pumpkin pie cravings this fall with these pumpkin-flavored truffles! These sugar-free fat bombs are finished with a quick roll in a sweet, cinnamon-spiced coating.

Ingredients

For the truffles:

½ cup (125 g/4.4 oz) coconut butter

¼ cup (55 g/2 oz) coconut oil

½ cup (100 g/3.5 oz) unsweetened pumpkin purée

2 teaspoons pumpkin pie spice mix

1 teaspoon sugar-free vanilla extract or ½ teaspoon vanilla powder

2 tablespoons (20 g/0.7 oz) powdered erythritol or Swerve

2 heaping tablespoons (24 g/0.8 oz) coconut flour

Pinch salt

Few drops liquid stevia, to taste (optional)

1 tablespoon (14 g/0.5 oz) macadamia oil or other light-tasting oil, for shaping the truffles

For the coating:

2 tablespoons (20 g/0.7 oz) powdered erythritol or Swerve

1½ teaspoons ground cinnamon

Instructions

To make the truffles: Melt the coconut butter and coconut oil in a double boiler, or heat-proof bowl placed over a small saucepan filled with 1 cup (235 ml/8 oz) of water, over medium heat. Remove from the heat and set aside.

Stir in the pumpkin purée, pumpkin pie spice mix, vanilla, erythritol or Swerve, coconut flour, and salt, until combined well. If you want a sweeter taste, add the stevia. Refrigerate for 30 minutes to 1 hour, or until firm enough to form truffles.

To shape the truffles, dip a spoon or melon baller in warm water and scoop out 10 balls of the chilled mixture. Lightly coat your hands in macadamia oil. Roll the truffles between your palms to form spheres about twice the size of standard truffles. Coat the truffles immediately after shaping.

To make the coating: In a bowl, mix together the erythritol or Swerve and cinnamon. Roll the truffles in the cinnamon mixture. Refrigerate the coated truffles for at least 15 minutes to harden. Keep in the refrigerator for up to 1 week or freeze for up to 3 months.

Nutrition facts per serving (1 truffle)

Total carbs:	Fiber:	Net carbs:	Protein:	Fat:	Energy:	Calories from:
6.4 g	**3 g**	**2 g**	**1.3 g**	**12.7 g**	**132 kcal**	**Carbs (6%)** **Protein (4%)** **Fat (90%)**

Yield:
10 truffles

Hands-on time:
15 mins

Overall time:
**15 mins +
chilling time**

Cookies and Cream Truffles

Incredibly smooth and creamy, these truffles are made with grain-free cookies—then doused in sugar-free white chocolate. They're nothing short of divine.

Ingredients

For the cookie:

½ cup (50 g/1.8 oz) almond flour

3 tablespoons (15 g/0.5 oz) unsweetened cacao powder

¼ cup (50 g/1.8 oz) granulated erythritol or Swerve

¼ teaspoon baking soda mixed with ½ teaspoon cream of tartar, or 1 teaspoon gluten-free baking powder

Pinch salt

1 large egg

1 tablespoon (14 g/0.5 oz) coconut oil

For the truffles

1 cookie, crumbled into small pieces (directions follow)

1 cup (240 g/8.5 oz) full-fat cream cheese or creamed coconut milk

2 tablespoons (20 g/0.7 oz) powdered erythritol or Swerve

1 teaspoon sugar-free vanilla extract or ½ teaspoon vanilla powder

Few drops liquid stevia, to taste (optional)

1 tablespoon (14 g/0.5 oz) macadamia oil or other light-tasting oil, for shaping the truffles

For the coating:

4.2 ounces (120 g) Homemade White Chocolate (page 34)

2 tablespoons (12 g/0.4 oz) crumbled cookie, for garnish

Nutrition facts per serving (1 truffle)

Total carbs:	Fiber:	Net carbs:	Protein:	Fat:	Energy:	Calories from:
3 g	**0.8 g**	**2.2 g**	**2.8 g**	**15.2 g**	**147 kcal**	**Carbs (6%)** **Protein (7%)** **Fat (87%)**

Yield:
14 truffles

Hands-on time:
20 mins

Overall time:
40 mins + chilling time

Instructions

If using creamed coconut milk, make it following the instructions on page 10.

To make the cookie: Preheat the oven to 300°F (150°C, or gas mark 2). In a mixing bowl, stir together the almond flour, cacao powder, erythritol or Swerve, baking soda and cream of tartar, and salt. Mix in the egg and coconut oil with your hands.

Place the dough on a sheet of parchment paper. Top with another sheet of parchment and roll out to create a large cookie about ¼ inch (6 mm) thick. Transfer to a baking sheet and place it in the preheated oven. Bake for 12 to 15 minutes, or until crispy. Cool to room temperature.

To make the truffles: Break the cookie into small pieces and place half in a food processor. Add the cream cheese or creamed coconut milk, erythritol or Swerve, and vanilla. Pulse until smooth. Set aside 2 tablespoons (12 g/0.4 oz) of cookie pieces for topping. Transfer the cookie/cream cheese mixture to a bowl. Stir in the remaining cookie pieces. For a sweeter taste, add the stevia and mix again. Refrigerate for 30 minutes to 1 hour, or until firm enough to form truffles.

To shape the truffles, use a spoon or melon baller to scoop out 14 balls of the chilled mixture. Lightly coat your hands in macadamia oil. Roll the truffles between your palms to form spheres about twice the size of standard truffles. Place on a parchment-lined tray and freeze for about 30 minutes.

To make the coating: Melt the white chocolate in a double boiler, or heat-proof bowl placed over a small saucepan filled with 1 cup (235 ml/8 oz) of water, over medium heat. Remove from the heat and set aside to cool.

Gently pierce each frozen truffle with a toothpick or a fork. Working one at a time, hold each truffle over the melted white chocolate and spoon the chocolate over it to coat completely. Turn the stick as you work until the coating is solidified. Place the coated truffles on a parchment-lined tray and drizzle any remaining coating over them. Before they become completely solid, sprinkle the truffles with the reserved crumbled cookies.

Refrigerate the coated truffles for at least 15 minutes to harden. Keep refrigerated for up to 1 week or freeze for up to 3 months.

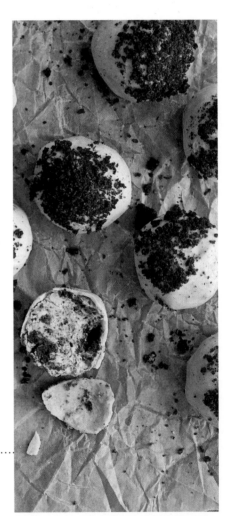

Gingerbread Truffles

These fat bombs are a lot like my Cookies and Cream Truffles on page 60—except they're packed with grain-free gingerbread cookies, which gives them a spicy, festive, wintery twist.

Ingredients

For the gingerbread cookie:

½ cup (50 g/1.8 oz) almond flour

1 heaping tablespoon (12 g/0.4 oz) coconut flour

3 tablespoons (30 g/1.1 oz) granulated erythritol or Swerve

1 tablespoon (8 g/0.3 oz) gingerbread spice mix

1 teaspoon sugar-free vanilla extract or ½ teaspoon vanilla powder

¼ teaspoon baking soda mixed with ½ teaspoon cream of tartar, or 1 teaspoon gluten-free baking powder

Pinch salt

1 large egg

1 tablespoon (14 g/0.5 oz) coconut oil

For the truffles:

Gingerbread cookie, crumbled into small pieces

1 cup (240 g/8.5 oz) full-fat cream cheese or creamed coconut milk

1 teaspoon ground ginger or 1 tablespoon (6 g/0.2 oz) grated fresh ginger

2 tablespoons (20 g /0.7 oz) powdered erythritol or Swerve

Few drops liquid stevia, to taste (optional)

1 tablespoon (14 g/0.5 oz) macadamia oil for shaping the truffles

For the coating:

4.2 ounces (120 g) Homemade White Chocolate (page 34)

2 tablespoons (12 g/0.4 oz) crumbled cookies, for garnish

Nutrition facts per serving (1 truffle)

Total carbs:	Fiber:	Net carbs:	Protein:	Fat:	Energy:	Calories from:
3.1 g	**0.9 g**	**2.2 g**	**2.2 g**	**15.2 g**	**149 kcal**	**Carbs (6%)** **Protein (7%)** **Fat (87%)**

Instructions

If using creamed coconut milk, make it following the instructions on page 10.

To make the cookie: Preheat the oven to 300°F (150°C, or gas mark 2). In a mixing bowl, stir together the almond flour, coconut flour, erythritol or Swerve, gingerbread spice mix, vanilla, baking soda and cream of tartar, and salt. Mix in the egg and coconut oil with your hands.

Place the dough on a sheet of parchment paper. Top with another sheet of parchment and roll out to create a large cookie about ¼ inch (6 mm) thick. Transfer to a baking sheet and place it in the preheated oven. Bake for 12 to 15 minutes or until crispy. Cool to room temperature.

To make the truffles: Break the cookie into small pieces and place half in a food processor. Add the cream cheese or creamed coconut milk and erythritol or Swerve. Pulse until smooth. Set aside 2 tablespoons (12 g/0.4 oz) of the cookie pieces for topping. Transfer the cookie/cream cheese mixture to a bowl. Stir in the remaining cookie pieces. If you want a sweeter taste, add the stevia and mix again. Refrigerate for 30 minutes to 1 hour, or until firm enough to form truffles.

To shape the truffles, use a spoon or a melon baller to scoop out 14 balls of the chilled mixture. Lightly coat your hands in macadamia oil. Roll the truffles between your palms to form spheres about twice the size of standard truffles. Place on a parchment-lined tray freeze for about 30 minutes.

To make the coating: Melt the white chocolate in a double boiler, or heat-proof bowl placed over a small saucepan filled with 1 cup (235 ml/8 oz) of water, over medium heat. Remove from the heat and set aside to cool.

Gently pierce each frozen truffle with a toothpick or a fork. Working one at a time, hold each truffle over the melted white chocolate and spoon the chocolate over it to coat completely. Turn the stick as you work until the coating is solidified. Place the coated truffles on a parchment-lined tray and drizzle any remaining coating over them. Before they become completely solid, sprinkle the truffles with the remaining 2 tablespoons crumbled cookies.

Refrigerate the coated truffles for at least 15 minutes to harden. Keep refrigerated for up to 1 week or freeze for up to 3 months.

Yield:
12 truffles

Hands-on time:
20 mins

Overall time:
**20 mins +
chilling time**

Lemon Cheesecake Truffles

You don't need to say good-bye to cheesecake just because you're eating low-carb! Grab one of these zingy Lemon Cheesecake Truffles as a quick pick-me-up.

Ingredients

For the truffles:

1 cup (240 g/8.5 oz) full-fat mascarpone cheese or cream cheese, or creamed coconut milk

2 tablespoons (30 ml/1 fl oz) freshly squeezed lemon juice

1 tablespoon (6 g/0.2 oz) freshly grated lemon zest

¼ cup (40 g/1.4 oz) powdered erythritol or Swerve

½ cup (50 g/1.8 oz) almond flour

Few drops liquid stevia, to taste (optional)

For the coating:

4.2 ounces (120 g) Homemade White Chocolate (page 34)

2 teaspoons cacao powder

Instructions

If using creamed coconut milk, make it following the instructions on page 10.

To make the truffles: In a bowl, mix together the mascarpone or cream cheese, lemon juice, lemon zest, and erythritol or Swerve. Add the almond flour and stir until well combined. If you want a sweeter taste, add the stevia and mix again.

Use a spoon to shape the mixture into 12 rounds about twice the size of standard truffles. Place them on a parchment-lined tray. Alternatively, use round cake pop molds for a truffle shape. Freeze for at least 1 hour.

To make the coating: Melt the white chocolate in a double boiler, or heat-proof bowl placed over a small saucepan filled with 1 cup (235 ml/8 oz) of water, over medium heat. Remove from the heat and set aside.

Gently pierce each frozen truffle with a toothpick or a fork. Working one at a time, hold each truffle over the melted white chocolate and spoon the chocolate over it to coat completely. Turn the stick as you work until the coating is solidified. Place the coated truffles on a parchment-lined tray. Mix the remaining coating with the cacao powder and drizzle over the truffles.

Refrigerate the coated truffles for at least 15 minutes to harden. Keep refrigerated for up to 1 week, or freeze for up to 3 months.

Nutrition facts per serving (1 truffle)

Total carbs:	Fiber:	Net carbs:	Protein:	Fat:	Energy:	Calories from:
2.7 g	**0.6 g**	**2.1 g**	**2.3 g**	**16.4 g**	**165 kcal**	**Carbs (5%)** **Protein (6%)** **Fat (89%)**

Key Lime Cheesecake Truffles

Citrus and dark chocolate are made for each other. You know what I mean if you've tried the classic orange and chocolate pairing—but if you've never matched dark chocolate with palate-lifting lime, you're in for a wonderful surprise.

Ingredients

For the truffles:

1 cup (240 g/8.5 oz) full-fat mascarpone cheese or cream cheese, or creamed coconut milk

2 tablespoons (30 ml/1 fl oz) freshly squeezed lime juice

1 tablespoon (6 g/0.2 oz) freshly grated lime zest

¼ cup (40 g/1.4 oz) powdered erythritol or Swerve

½ cup (50 g/1.8 oz) almond flour

Few drops liquid stevia, to taste (optional)

For the coating (or use any of the Homemade Dark Chocolate recipes [page 32]):

2.5 ounces (70 g) extra-dark 90 percent chocolate

1 ounce (28 g) cacao butter

Instructions

If using creamed coconut milk, make it following the instructions on page 10.

To make and coat the truffles: Follow the steps for Lemon Cheesecake Truffles on page 65, but use lime juice and lime zest instead of lemon, and cover in dark chocolate.

To make the coating: Melt the dark chocolate and cacao butter in a double boiler, or heat-proof bowl placed over a small saucepan filled with 1 cup (235 ml/8 oz) of water, over medium heat. Remove from the heat and set aside to cool. If you are using any of the Homemade Dark Chocolate recipes (page 32), you may need as much as 4.6 to 4.9 ounces (130 to 140 g) to coat all the fat bombs.

Nutrition facts per serving (1 truffle)

Total carbs:	Fiber:	Net carbs:	Protein:	Fat:	Energy:	Calories from:
2.7 g	**0.9 g**	**1.8 g**	**2.6 g**	**14.9 g**	**150 kcal**	**Carbs (5%)** **Protein (7%)** **Fat (88%)**

Yield:
12 truffles

Hands-on time:
20 mins

Overall time:
**20 mins +
chilling time**

Chocolate and Raspberry Truffles

Raspberry and dark chocolate make a killer combination: the fruity tang of the berry is tamed when it's wrapped in a velvety cloak of chocolate. Pure indulgence—just like these soft, creamy, low-carb truffles.

Ingredients

For the truffles:

1 cup (240 g/8.5 oz) full-fat mascarpone cheese or cream cheese, or creamed coconut milk

¼ cup (60 ml/2 fl oz) heavy whipping cream or coconut milk

¼ cup plus 1 tablespoon (50 g/1.8 oz) powdered erythritol or Swerve

½ cup (50 g/1.8 oz) almond flour

⅓ cup (30 g/1.1 oz) unsweetened cacao powder

Few drops liquid stevia, to taste (optional)

16 frozen raspberries (50 g/1.8 oz)

For the coating (or use any of the Homemade Dark Chocolate recipes [page 32]):

2.8 ounces (80 g) extra-dark 90 percent chocolate

1.4 ounces (40 g) cacao butter

Instructions

If using creamed coconut milk, make it following the instructions on page 10.

To make the truffles: In a bowl, mix together the mascarpone or cream cheese, cream or coconut milk, and erythritol or Swerve. Add the almond flour and cacao powder and mix until well combined. If you want a sweeter taste, add the stevia and mix again.

Use a 1-ounce (30 g) scoop to portion 16 mounds of the mixture on a parchment-lined tray. Press a raspberry into the top of each. Freeze for at least 1 hour.

To make the coating: Melt the dark chocolate and cacao butter in a double boiler, or heat-proof bowl placed over a small saucepan filled with 1 cup (235 ml/8 oz) of water, over medium heat. Remove from the heat and set aside to cool.

Gently pierce each frozen truffle with a toothpick or a fork. Working one at a time, hold each truffle over the melted dark chocolate and spoon the chocolate over it to coat completely. Turn the stick as you work until the coating is solidified. Place the coated truffles on a parchment-lined tray.

Refrigerate the coated truffles for at least 15 minutes to harden. Keep refrigerated for up to 5 days or freeze for up to 3 months.

Nutrition facts per serving (1 truffle)

Total carbs:	Fiber:	Net carbs:	Protein:	Fat:	Energy:	Calories from:
3.3 g	**1.3 g**	**1.9 g**	**2.5 g**	**14 g**	**140 kcal**	**Carbs (5%)** **Protein (7%)** **Fat (88%)**

Yield:
16 truffles

Hands-on time:
20 mins

Overall time:
20 mins + chilling time

Sweet and Savory Fat Bombs

Yield:
10 bars

Hands-on time:
20 mins

Overall time:
**20 mins +
chilling time**

Almond Bliss Bars

Chocolate and coconut: it's like the perfect island wedding. Add almonds, and it's the perfect love triangle! These sugar-free bars are absolutely irresistible and make a great post-workout snack.

Ingredients

For the bars:

½ cup (120 g/4.2 oz) creamed coconut milk

1½ cups (112 g/4 oz) unsweetened shredded coconut

¼ cup (55 g/1.9 oz) coconut oil, at room temperature

2 tablespoons (20 g/0.7 oz) powdered erythritol or Swerve

2 teaspoons sugar-free vanilla extract or 1 teaspoon vanilla powder

Pinch salt

Few drops liquid stevia, to taste (optional)

20 whole almonds (24 g/0.8 oz)

For the coating (or use any of the Homemade Dark Chocolate recipes [page 32]):

2 ounces (56 g) extra-dark 90 percent chocolate

0.8 ounces (24 g) cacao butter

Instructions

To make creamed coconut milk, follow the instructions on page 10.

To make the bars: In a mixing bowl, stir together the creamed coconut milk, shredded coconut, coconut oil, erythritol or Swerve, vanilla, and salt. If you want a sweeter taste, add the stevia and mix again. Use your hands to form the mixture into 10 small bars, about 1 ounce (32 g) each, and place them on a parchment-lined tray. Top each bar with 2 almonds. Freeze for about 30 minutes.

To make the coating: Melt the dark chocolate and cacao butter in a double boiler, or heat-proof bowl placed over a small saucepan filled with 1 cup (235 ml/ 8 oz) of water, over medium heat. Remove from the heat and set aside to cool.

Gently pierce each bar with a toothpick or a fork. Working one at a time, hold each bar over the melted dark chocolate and spoon the chocolate over it to coat completely. Turn the stick as you work until the coating is solidified. Place the coated bars on a parchment-lined tray and drizzle any remaining coating over them.

Refrigerate the coated bars for at least 15 minutes to harden. Keep refrigerated for up to 1 week or freeze for up to 3 months.

Nutrition facts per serving (1 bar)

Total carbs:	Fiber:	Net carbs:	Protein:	Fat:	Energy:	Calories from:
5.3 g	**2.8 g**	**2.5 g**	**3.8 g**	**17.8 g**	**193 kcal**	**Carbs (5%)** **Protein (8%)** **Fat (87%)**

Chocolate Cherry-Coconut Bars

Skip the store-bought, processed version of these bars, and make your own instead! They're so easy, and so much healthier. Experiment with different flavors. This recipe calls for cherry extract, but you can also use lemon or orange peel, cinnamon, or even turmeric. If you try any of these alternatives though, leave out the beetroot powder.

Ingredients

For bars:

1½ cups (112 g/4 oz) unsweetened shredded coconut

½ cup (120 g/4.2 oz) creamed coconut milk

¼ cup (55 g/1.9 oz) coconut oil, at room temperature

2 tablespoons (20 g/0.7 oz) powdered erythritol or Swerve

2 teaspoons sugar-free cherry extract

1 teaspoon sugar-free vanilla extract or ½ teaspoon vanilla powder

1 tablespoon (6 g/0.2 oz) beetroot powder

Pinch salt

Few drops liquid stevia, to taste (optional)

For coating (or use any of the Homemade Dark Chocolate recipes [page 32]):

2 ounces (56 g) extra-dark 90 percent chocolate

0.8 ounces (24 g) cacao butter

Instructions

To make creamed coconut milk, follow the instructions on page 10.

To make the bars: In a mixing bowl, mix together the shredded coconut, creamed coconut milk, coconut oil, erythritol or Swerve, cherry extract, vanilla, beetroot powder, and salt. If you want a sweeter taste, add the stevia and mix again. Use your hands to form the mixture into 10 small bars, about 1 ounce (32 g) each, and place them on a parchment-lined tray. Freeze for about 30 minutes.

To make the coating: Follow the steps for Almond Bliss Bars on page 71.

Nutrition facts per serving (1 bar)

Total carbs:	Fiber:	Net carbs:	Protein:	Fat:	Energy:	Calories from:
5.3 g	**2.6 g**	**2.7 g**	**3.3 g**	**16.7 g**	**183 kcal**	**Carbs (6%)** **Protein (8%)** **Fat (86%)**

Yield:
10 bars

Hands-on time:
20 mins

Overall time:
**20 mins +
chilling time**

Raspberry and Dark Chocolate Cups

Chocolate, raspberries, and crunchy almonds live together in perfect harmony in these fabulous low-carb treats.

Ingredients

16 whole almonds
(20 g/0.7 oz)

16 fresh raspberries
(80 g/2.8 oz)

7.8 ounces (220 g) Homemade
Dark Chocolate (page 32)

1 tablespoon (14 g/0.5 oz)
coconut oil

Instructions

Place the almonds in a dry skillet set over medium-high heat and dry-fry for 3 to 5 minutes to enhance their flavor. Insert 1 almond into the "cup" of each raspberry and place them on a tray. Freeze for about 1 hour. (Freezing isn't essential, but it does help the chocolate solidify faster.)

Melt the dark chocolate and coconut oil in a double boiler, or heat-proof bowl placed over a small saucepan filled with 1 cup (235 ml/8 oz) of water, over medium heat. Once melted, remove from the heat and cool until it is not hot but still liquid.

Place 8 small paper muffin cups on a tray. Pour about 1 tablespoon (13 g/0.45 oz) of chocolate into each. Add 2 almond-filled raspberries to each cup. Pour another 1 tablespoon (15 g/0.5 oz) of chocolate over the berries in each cup, making sure they are completely covered. The chocolate will start to solidify instantly if the berries were frozen.

Refrigerate for about 30 minutes, or until set. Keep refrigerated for up to 3 days or freeze for up to 3 months.

Nutrition facts per serving (1 fat bomb)

Total carbs:	Fiber:	Net carbs:	Protein:	Fat:	Energy:	Calories from:
4.7 g	**2.4 g**	**2.3 g**	**2.1 g**	**18.9 g**	**195 kcal**	**Carbs (5%)** **Protein (4%)** **Fat (91%)**

Note: Nutritional facts are calculated using Homemade Dark Chocolate made with unsweetened chocolate (see recipe on page 32).

Yield:
8 fat bombs

Hands-on time:
10 mins

Overall time:
**10 mins +
chilling time**

Cookie Dough Cups

If you've got ten minutes and a batch each of my Homemade Dark Chocolate
(page 32) and Chocolate Chip Cookie Butter (page 28), you have everything
you need to make these satisfying fat bombs and put a smile on your face.

Ingredients

3.5 ounces (100 g) Homemade
Dark Chocolate (page 32)

1 cup (250 g/8.3 oz) Chocolate
Chip Cookie Butter (page 28)

Instructions

Melt the dark chocolate in a double boiler, or heat-
proof bowl placed over a small saucepan filled with
1 cup (235 ml/8 oz) of water, over medium heat.
Remove from the heat and cool slightly.

Place 8 small paper muffin cups on a tray. Pour
1 tablespoon (13 g/0.45 oz) of chocolate into each.
Refrigerate for about 15 minutes to harden. When
solid, top each cup with about 2 tablespoons (30 g/
1 oz) of cookie butter.

Refrigerate for about 30 minutes, or until set.
Keep refrigerated for up to 1 week or freeze for up
to 3 months.

Nutrition facts per serving (1 fat bomb)

Total carbs:	Fiber:	Net carbs:	Protein:	Fat:	Energy:	Calories from:
5.2 g	**2.1 g**	**3.1 g**	**3.9 g**	**23.5 g**	**240 kcal**	**Carbs (5%)** **Protein (7%)** **Fat (88%)**

Note: Nutritional facts are calculated using Homemade Dark Chocolate made with unsweetened chocolate (see recipe on page 32).

Yield:
12 fat bombs

Hands-on time:
15 mins

Overall time:
15 mins + chilling time

Toasted Coconut Cups

This is one of the most popular recipes on my blog—not the least because it's surprisingly easy to make! Toasting the coconut brings out its natural sweetness and adds some crunch.

Ingredients

1½ cups (112 g/4 oz) unsweetened desiccated, shredded, or flaked coconut

¼ cup (55 g/1.9 oz) extra virgin coconut oil, at room temperature

¼ cup (56 g/2 oz) unsalted butter, or more coconut oil, at room temperature

¼ teaspoon ground cinnamon or vanilla powder

Pinch salt

Few drops liquid stevia, to taste, or 2 tablespoons (20 g/0.7 oz) powdered erythritol or Swerve (optional)

Instructions

Preheat the oven to 350°F (175°C, or gas mark 4). Spread the coconut on a baking sheet. Place it in the preheated oven and toast for 5 to 8 minutes, or until lightly golden. Stir once or twice to prevent burning. Remove from the oven and cool for 5 minutes. Transfer to a food processor and pulse until smooth. This may take time. At first, the mixture will be dry. Scrape down the sides of your processor several times with a rubber spatula if the mixture sticks. The final consistency should be smooth and runny.

Add the coconut oil. Then add the butter 2 tablespoons at a time, pulsing after each addition. Add the cinnamon or vanilla powder and salt. Pulse to mix well. If you want a sweeter taste, add the stevia and pulse again.

Fill a mini muffin tin or ice cube tray with 2-tablespoon (20 g/0.7 oz) portions. Refrigerate for at least 30 minutes, or until solid. Keep refrigerated for up to 1 week, as the coconut oil and butter become very soft at room temperature, or freeze for up to 3 months.

Nutrition facts per serving (1 fat bomb)

Total carbs:	Fiber:	Net carbs:	Protein:	Fat:	Energy:	Calories from:
2.6 g	**1.9 g**	**0.7 g**	**1.9 g**	**9.6 g**	**104 kcal**	**Carbs (3%)** **Protein (8%)** **Fat (89%)**

Chocolate and Mint Cups

Those chocolatey, sugar-laden after-dinner mints that you used to love? You'll never crave one again once you've tried these sugar-free fat bombs. Best of all, they're as simple to make as the Toasted Coconut Cups on page 77.

Ingredients

7.1 ounces (200 g) coconut butter

¼ cup (55 g/1.9 oz) coconut oil

¼ cup (56 g/2 oz) unsalted butter, ghee, or more coconut oil, at room temperature

¼ cup (40 g/1.4 oz) powdered erythritol or Swerve

2 tablespoons (12 g/0.4 oz) chopped fresh mint leaves or 1 teaspoon peppermint extract

⅓ cup (30 g/1.1 oz) unsweetened cacao powder

Pinch salt

Few drops liquid stevia, to taste (optional)

Instructions

Melt the coconut butter and coconut oil in a double boiler, or heat-proof bowl placed over a small saucepan filled with 1 cup (240 ml/8.1 fl oz) of water, over medium heat. Remove from the heat and add the butter, ghee, or oil, stirring until the butter is completely melted. Mix in the erythritol or Swerve. Transfer about a third of the mixture in another bowl and mix with the peppermint extract. Combine the remaining two-thirds of the coconut butter mixture with cacao powder, salt, and stevia.

If using mint leaves: Transfer about one-third of the coconut mixture to a food processor or a blender, leaving the remaining two-thirds in the bowl. Add the mint leaves and process until smooth.

To make the fat bombs: Fill 9 small muffin cups with about 1 tablespoon (15 g/0.5 oz) of the chocolate mixture. Refrigerate for 5 minutes. Top each with about 1 tablespoon (15 g/0.5 oz) of the mint-chocolate mixture. Refrigerate for 5 minutes more. Add a final 1-tablespoon (15 g/0.5 oz) layer of the chocolate mixture. Refrigerate again for 30 minutes to 1 hour, or until solid.

Keep refrigerated up to 1 week, as the coconut oil and butter become very soft at room temperature, or freeze for up to 3 months.

Nutrition facts per serving (1 fat bomb)

Total carbs:	Fiber:	Net carbs:	Protein:	Fat:	Energy:	Calories from:
6.8 g	**4.4 g**	**2.4 g**	**2 g**	**23.9 g**	**232 kcal**	**Carbs (4%)** **Protein (4%)** **Fat (92%)**

Yield:	Hands-on time:	Overall time:
12 fat bombs	**15 mins**	**15 mins +** **chilling time**

Chocolate and Berry Cups

A layer of rich Berry Nut Butter (page 24) sandwiched between two layers of dark chocolate? Bring it on.

Ingredients

10.6 ounces (300 g)
Homemade Dark Chocolate
(page 32)

½ recipe (250 g/8.8 oz) Berry
Nut Butter (page 24)

Instructions

Melt the dark chocolate in a double boiler, or heat-proof bowl placed over a small saucepan filled with 1 cup (235 ml/8 oz) of water, over medium heat. Remove from the heat and cool slightly.

Place 12 small paper muffin cups on a tray. Pour 1 tablespoon (13 g/0.45 oz) of chocolate into each. Refrigerate for about 30 minutes to harden.

When solid, top each cup with 1 heaping tablespoon (20 g/0.7 oz) of Berry Nut Butter. Divide the remaining chocolate among the cups. Refrigerate for about 30 minutes, or until solid. Keep refrigerated for up to 1 week or freeze for up to 3 months.

Nutrition facts per serving (1 fat bomb)

Total carbs:	Fiber:	Net carbs:	Protein:	Fat:	Energy:	Calories from:
6.8 g	**3.7 g**	**3.1 g**	**3.2 g**	**27.3 g**	**275 kcal**	**Carbs (5%)** **Protein (5%)** **Fat (90%)**

Note: Nutritional facts are calculated using Homemade Dark Chocolate made with unsweetened chocolate (see recipe on page 32).

Yield:
10 fat bombs

Hands-on time:
30 mins

Overall time:
45 mins + chilling time

Salted-Caramel Chocolate Cups

This is one of my hands-down favorites. The salted-caramel filling lurking in its dark chocolate coating tastes like caramel and marzipan rolled into one. Magic.

Ingredients

For caramel filling (you'll use half a batch in this recipe):

1 cup (240 ml/8 fl oz) coconut milk or heavy whipping cream

½ cup (80 g/1.8 oz) powdered erythritol or Swerve

½ cup (130 g/4.6 oz) almond butter or Almond and Cashew Butter (page 16)

½ to 1 teaspoon salt, plus more for topping

Few drops liquid stevia, to taste (optional)

For chocolate coating:

10 ounces (280 g) Homemade Dark Chocolate (page 32)

Instructions

To make the caramel filling: In a small saucepan set over medium heat, bring the coconut milk or heavy cream to a boil. Once simmering, reduce the heat to low. Stir in the erythritol or Swerve. Cook for 10 to 15 minutes, stirring occasionally, until the milk is creamy and reduced by about half. Remove from the heat and stir in the nut butter and salt until creamy and smooth. If you want a sweeter taste, add the stevia and mix again. Cool for a few minutes.

Transfer half of the mixture to a small bowl and refrigerate for 30 minutes to 1 hour. Place the other half in a freezer-safe jar and freeze for another batch.

To make the coating: Melt the dark chocolate in a double boiler, or heat-proof bowl placed over a small saucepan filled with 1 cup (235 ml/8 oz) of water, over medium heat. Remove from the heat and cool slightly.

Place 10 small paper muffin cups on a tray. Fill each with 1 tablespoon (13 g/0.45 oz) of chocolate. Refrigerate for about 15 minutes to harden.

When the chocolate is solid, top each cup with 1 tablespoon (15 g/0.5 oz) of the caramel mixture. Pour another 1 tablespoon (13 g/0.45 oz) of chocolate in each cup. Refrigerate for 30 minutes to 1 hour, or until solid. Keep the fat bombs refrigerated for up to 1 week or freeze for up to 3 months.

Nutrition facts per serving (1 fat bomb)

Total carbs:	Fiber:	Net carbs:	Protein:	Fat:	Energy:	Calories from:
4.9 g	**2.4 g**	**2.5 g**	**3 g**	**22.4 g**	**236 kcal**	**Carbs (5%)** **Protein (5%)** **Fat (90%)**

Note: Nutritional facts are calculated using Homemade Dark Chocolate made with unsweetened chocolate (see recipe on page 32).

Lemon and Green Tea Cups

Matcha, or powdered green tea, is full of health benefits: it's high in antioxidants and has been said to improve mental clarity. It's also a natural partner for lemon, as in these sugar-free fat bombs.

Ingredients

½ cup (65 g/2.3 oz) macadamia nuts

½ cup (125 g/4.4 oz) coconut butter

½ cup (110 g/3.8 oz) cacao butter

¼ cup (55 g/1.9 oz) coconut oil

¼ cup (40 g/1.4 oz) powdered erythritol or Swerve

Few drops liquid stevia, to taste (optional)

1 teaspoon matcha green tea powder

1 tablespoon (6 g/0.2 oz) freshly grated lemon zest

Instructions

In a food processor, combine the macadamia nuts, coconut butter, cacao butter, coconut oil, and erythritol or Swerve. Pulse for 30 to 60 seconds, or until smooth. If you want a sweeter taste, add the stevia and pulse to combine.

Divide the mixture in half between 2 bowls. Stir the matcha powder into one half; stir the lemon zest into the other half.

Place 10 small paper muffin cups on a tray. Fill each with about 1½ tablespoons (20 g/0.7 oz) of the matcha mixture. Top with another 1½ tablespoons (20 g/0.7 oz) of the lemon mixture. Refrigerate for 30 minutes to 1 hour, or until solid. Keep refrigerated for up to 1 week or freeze for up to 3 months.

Nutrition facts per serving (1 fat bomb)

Total carbs:	Fiber:	Net carbs:	Protein:	Fat:	Energy:	Calories from:
4.2 g	**2.8 g**	**1.4 g**	**1.3 g**	**28.2 g**	**261 kcal**	**Carbs (2%)** **Protein (2%)** **Fat (96%)**

Yield:
10 fat bombs

Hands-on time:
15 mins

Overall time:
**15 mins +
chilling time**

Yield:
16 fat bombs

Hands-on time:
15 mins

Overall time:
**15 mins +
chilling time**

Chocolate Brownie Fudge

Decadent yet guilt-free (honestly!), these dark chocolate brownie squares
are great for keeping sugar cravings at bay.

Ingredients

5.3 ounces (150 g) Homemade
Dark Chocolate (page 32)

2 ounces (56 g) cacao butter

½ cup (40 g/1.4 oz)
unsweetened cacao powder

½ cup (50 g/1.7 oz) powdered
erythritol or Swerve

½ cup (120 g/4.2 oz) creamed
coconut milk

½ cup (112 g/4 oz) unsalted
butter or coconut oil, at room
temperature

Pinch salt

Few drops liquid stevia, to taste
(optional)

1 cup (100 g/3.5 oz) almond
flour

Instructions

To make creamed coconut milk, follow the instructions
on page 10.

Melt the dark chocolate and cacao butter in a
double boiler, or heat-proof bowl placed over a small
saucepan filled with 1 cup (235 ml/8 oz) of water, over
medium heat. Stir in the cacao powder and erythritol
or Swerve and then remove from the heat. Stir in the
creamed coconut milk and butter or oil. Add the salt
and mix until well combined. If you want a sweeter
taste, add the stevia and mix again.

Add the almond flour and combine well. Transfer
the dough to an 8 x 8-inch (20 x 20 cm) parchment-
lined pan, or a silicone pan. With a spatula, spread
the dough evenly into the pan. Refrigerate for 1 to
2 hours, or until set. Be sure the brownies have set
before slicing. Keep refrigerated for up to 1 week or
freeze for up to 3 months.

Nutrition facts per serving (1 fat bomb)

Total carbs:	Fiber:	Net carbs:	Protein:	Fat:	Energy:	Calories from:
4.3 g	**2 g**	**2.2 g**	**2.7 g**	**20.9 g**	**205 kcal**	**Carbs (4%)** **Protein (5%)** **Fat (91%)**

Note: Nutritional facts are calculated using Homemade Dark Chocolate made with unsweetened chocolate (see recipe on page 32).

Yield:
16 fat bombs

Hands-on time:
10 mins

Overall time:
**10 mins +
chilling time**

White Chocolate and Macadamia Fudge

Crunchy, creamy, and laced with good-for-you macadamia nuts, this white chocolate fudge is sure to satisfy even the most wicked sweet tooth.

Ingredients

1 recipe (410 g/14.5 oz) White Chocolate and Macadamia Butter (page 23)

2 tablespoons (20 g/0.7 oz) powdered erythritol or Swerve

⅓ cup (75 g/2.6 oz) unsalted butter or coconut oil, at room temperature

2 teaspoons sugar-free vanilla extract or 1 teaspoon vanilla powder

Few drops liquid stevia, to taste (optional)

1¼ cups (160 g/5.6 oz) macadamia nuts, roughly chopped

Instructions

In a food processor, combine the White Chocolate and Macadamia Butter, erythritol or Swerve, butter or oil, and vanilla. Pulse until smooth. If you want a sweeter taste, add the stevia and pulse again.

Add the macadamia nuts and combine well. Transfer the dough to an 8 x 8-inch (20 x 20 cm) parchment-lined pan, or a silicone pan. With a spatula, spread the dough evenly into the pan. Refrigerate for 1 to 2 hours, or until set. Be sure the fudge has set before slicing. Keep refrigerated for up to 1 week or freeze for up to 3 months.

Nutrition facts per serving (1 fat bomb)

Total carbs:	Fiber:	Net carbs:	Protein:	Fat:	Energy:	Calories from:
4.4 g	**2.8 g**	**1.7 g**	**2 g**	**28.9 g**	**273 kcal**	**Carbs (2%)** **Protein (3%)** **Fat (95%)**

Yield:
16 fat bombs

Hands-on time:
10 mins

Overall time:
**10 mins +
chilling time**

Maple and Pecan Fudge

**These bite-size fat bombs remind me of pecan pie—the last word in comfort food.
They're just as delicious, and they're sure to keep you sated until your next meal.**

Ingredients

1 recipe (310 g/10.9 oz) Spiced Maple and Pecan Butter (page 26)

¼ cup (40 g/1.4 oz) powdered erythritol or Swerve

½ cup (112 g/4 oz) unsalted butter or coconut oil, at room temperature

Pinch salt

Few drops liquid stevia, to taste (optional)

1½ cups (150 g/5.3 oz) pecans, halved

Instructions

In a food processor, combine the Spiced Maple and Pecan Butter, erythritol or Swerve, butter or oil, and salt. Pulse until smooth. If you want a sweeter taste, add the stevia and pulse again.

Transfer the dough to an 8 x 8-inch (20 x 20 cm) parchment-lined pan, or a silicone pan. With a spatula, spread the dough evenly into the pan. Top with the pecan halves. Refrigerate for 1 to 2 hours, or until set. Be sure the fudge has set before slicing. Keep refrigerated for up to 1 week or freeze for up to 3 months.

Nutrition facts per serving (1 fat bomb)

Total carbs:	Fiber:	Net carbs:	Protein:	Fat:	Energy:	Calories from:
4.2 g	**2.8 g**	**1.4 g**	**2.6 g**	**26 g**	**247 kcal**	**Carbs (2%)** **Protein (4%)** **Fat (94%)**

Yield:	Hands-on time:	Overall time:
16 fat bombs	**20 mins**	**20 mins + chilling time**

Mexican Chili-Chocolate Fudge

Made with homemade dark chocolate and ripe avocados, this creamy chocolate fudge is loaded with good fats, plus a dash of cayenne pepper. Don't worry: the dark chocolate tames the heat! All you taste is delicious.

Ingredients

4.2 ounces (120 g) Homemade Dark Chocolate (page 32)

¼ cup (60 ml/2 fl oz) strong brewed coffee or 1 teaspoon instant coffee granules

½ cup (40 g/1.4 oz) unsweetened cacao powder

¼ cup plus 1 tablespoon (50 g /1.8 oz) powdered erythritol or Swerve

1 teaspoon sugar-free vanilla extract or ½ teaspoon vanilla powder

¼ to ½ teaspoon cayenne pepper

Pinch salt

½ cup (112 g/4 oz) unsalted butter or coconut oil, at room temperature

2 medium (300 g/10.6 oz) ripe avocados, halved and pitted

Few drops liquid stevia, to taste (optional)

Instructions

Melt the dark chocolate in a double boiler, or heat-proof bowl placed over a small saucepan filled with 1 cup (235 ml/8 oz) of water, over medium heat. Slowly stir in the coffee. Add cacao powder, erythritol or Swerve, vanilla, cayenne pepper, and salt and stir to combine. Remove from the heat. Add the butter or oil and stir until smooth and creamy.

Scoop the avocado flesh into a food processor and pulse until smooth. With the processor running, add the chocolate mixture. If you want a sweeter taste, add the stevia and pulse to combine.

Transfer the dough to an 8 x 8-inch (20 x 20 cm) parchment-lined pan, or a silicone pan. With a spatula, spread the dough evenly into the pan. Refrigerate for 1 to 2 hours, or until set. Be sure the fudge has set before slicing. Keep refrigerated for up to 1 week or freeze for up to 3 months.

Nutrition facts per serving (1 fat bomb)

Total carbs:	Fiber:	Net carbs:	Protein:	Fat:	Energy:	Calories from:
4.1 g	**2.5 g**	**1.6 g**	**1.3 g**	**13.2 g**	**132 kcal**	**Carbs (5%)** **Protein (4%)** **Fat (91%)**

Note: Nutritional facts are calculated using Homemade Dark Chocolate made with unsweetened chocolate (see recipe on page 32).

Dulce de Leche Squares

Using homemade "condensed milk" in this recipe ensures these naturally sweet fat bombs are dairy-free, low in carbs, and high in healthy fats.

Ingredients

For the squares:

1½ cups (112 g/4 oz) unsweetened shredded coconut

1¼ cups (160 g/5.6 oz) macadamia nuts, chopped

1 can (400 ml/13.5 fl oz) coconut milk or equivalent amount of heavy whipping cream

¼ cup (40 g/1.4 oz) powdered erythritol or Swerve

2 teaspoons sugar-free vanilla extract or 1 teaspoon vanilla powder

¼ cup (55 g/1.9 oz) coconut oil, at room temperature

Few drops liquid stevia, to taste (optional)

For the coating:

2 ounces (56 g) Homemade Dark Chocolate (page 32)

Instructions

To make the squares: Preheat the oven to 350°F (175°C, or gas mark 4). Spread the coconut and macadamia nuts on a baking sheet. Place it in the preheated oven and toast for 5 to 8 minutes, or until lightly golden. Stir once or twice to prevent burning. Remove from the oven and set aside.

To make the condensed milk: In a small saucepan set over medium heat, bring the coconut milk or heavy cream to a boil. Once simmering, reduce the heat to low. Stir in the erythritol or Swerve and vanilla, stirring until the erythritol is dissolved. Cook for 20 to 30 minutes, stirring occasionally, until the milk is creamy and reduced by about half. Remove from the heat and cool.

To a mixing bowl, add the toasted coconut and macadamia nuts. Pour the condensed coconut milk over them. Add the coconut oil and mix until well combined. If you want a sweeter taste, add the stevia and mix again.

Nutrition facts per serving (1 fat bomb)

Total carbs:	Fiber:	Net carbs:	Protein:	Fat:	Energy:	Calories from:
4.3 g	**2.2 g**	**2.1 g**	**2.8 g**	**19.3 g**	**194 kcal**	**Carbs (4%)** **Protein (6%)** **Fat (90%)**

Note: Nutritional facts are calculated using Homemade Dark Chocolate made with unsweetened chocolate (see recipe on page 32).

Yield:
16 fat bombs

Hands-on time:
20 mins

Overall time:
**40 mins +
chilling time**

Transfer the dough to an 8 x 8-inch (20 x 20 cm) parchment-lined pan, or a silicone pan. With a spatula, spread the dough evenly in the pan. Refrigerate for 30 to 45 minutes.

To make the coating: Melt the dark chocolate in a double boiler, or heat-proof bowl placed over a small saucepan filled with 1 cup (235 ml/8 oz) of water, over medium heat. Drizzle the chilled coconut mixture with the melted dark chocolate. Return to the refrigerator for 15 minutes to set before slicing. Keep refrigerated for up to 1 week or freeze for up to 3 months.

Pistachio-Coconut Squares

Coconut, pistachio, and vanilla form a happy trio here. Scatter these squares with a couple handfuls of whole pistachios while they're still in the pan to add a gratifying layer of crunch.

Ingredients

1 cup (250 g/8.8 oz) coconut butter, at room temperature (see Tip)

¼ cup (55 g/1.9 oz) coconut oil, at room temperature

2 tablespoons (20 g/0.7 oz) powdered erythritol or Swerve

2 teaspoons sugar-free vanilla extract or 1 teaspoon vanilla powder

Few drops liquid stevia, to taste (optional)

1 recipe (330 g/11.6) Pistachio-Coconut Butter (page 30), at room temperature

½ cup (60 g/2.1 oz) unsalted pistachio nuts, raw or roasted

Instructions

In a mixing bowl, mix together the coconut butter, coconut oil, erythritol or Swerve, and vanilla. If you want a sweeter taste, add the stevia and mix again.

Transfer the dough to an 8 x 8-inch (20 x 20 cm) parchment-lined pan, or a silicone pan. With a spatula, spread the mixture evenly in the pan. Top with the Pistachio-Coconut Butter and sprinkle with the pistachios. Refrigerate for 1 to 2 hours, or until set. Be sure the dough has set before slicing. Keep refrigerated for up to 1 week or freeze for up to 3 months.

Nutrition facts per serving (1 fat bomb)

Total carbs:	Fiber:	Net carbs:	Protein:	Fat:	Energy:	Calories from:
8.8 g	**5 g**	**3.8 g**	**4.8 g**	**23.9 g**	**257 kcal**	**Carbs (8%)** **Protein (6%)** **Fat (86%)**

Yield:
16 fat bombs

Hands-on time:
15 mins

Overall time:
**15 mins +
chilling time**

Tip

Regular coconut butter works fine here, but you can add an extra dimension of flavor by using coconut butter made with toasted desiccated coconut.

To make toasted coconut, preheat the oven to 350°F (175°C, or gas mark 4). Spread about 4 cups (280 g/9.9 oz) of the shredded (or flaked) coconut over 2 or 3 baking sheets.

Place in the oven and toast for 5 to 8 minutes until light golden. Mix once or twice to prevent burning.

Yield:
16 fat bombs

Hands-on time:
20 mins

Overall time:
**20 mins +
chilling time**

Chewy Hempseed Squares

Hempseeds are low in carbohydrates and high in protein and healthy fats, so they're perfect for making nut-free fat bombs. These sweet, sugar-free squares are bound with homemade condensed milk and framed by thin layers of chocolate.

Ingredients

For squares:

1 can (400 ml/13.5 fl oz) coconut milk or equivalent amount of heavy whipping cream

¼ cup (40 g/1.4 oz) powdered erythritol or Swerve

2 teaspoons sugar-free vanilla extract or 1 teaspoon vanilla powder

1 teaspoon ground cinnamon

¼ cup (55 g/1.9 oz) coconut oil

2 tablespoons (16 g/0.6 oz) ground chia seeds

1½ cups (210 g/7.4 oz) hempseeds, hulled

Few drops liquid stevia, to taste (optional)

For coating:

7.1 ounces (200 g) Homemade Dark Chocolate (page 32)

Instructions

To make the squares: In a small saucepan set over medium heat, bring the coconut milk or heavy cream to a boil. Once simmering, reduce the heat to low. Stir in the erythritol or Swerve, vanilla, and cinnamon, stirring until the erythritol is dissolved. Cook for 20 to 30 minutes, stirring occasionally, until the milk is creamy and reduced by about half. Remove from the heat and mix in the coconut oil, chia seeds, and hempseeds. If you want a sweeter taste, add the stevia and mix again. Let the mixture sit for 5 to 10 minutes, then refrigerate for about 30 minutes.

To make the coating: Melt the dark chocolate in a double boiler, or heat-proof bowl placed over a small saucepan filled with 1 cup (235 ml/8 oz) of water, over medium heat. Pour half into an 8 x 8-inch (20 x 20 cm) parchment-lined pan, or a silicone pan. With a spatula, spread the chocolate over the bottom of the pan. Refrigerate for about 15 minutes, or until hardened. Reserve the other half of the melted chocolate for topping.

Remove both the chocolate and hempseed mixtures from the refrigerator. With a spatula, spread and flatten the hempseed mixture over the chilled chocolate mixture. Top with the remaining melted chocolate. Refrigerate for 45 to 60 minutes to set before slicing. Keep refrigerated for up to 1 week or freeze for up to 3 months.

Nutrition facts per serving (1 fat bomb)

Total carbs:	Fiber:	Net carbs:	Protein:	Fat:	Energy:	Calories from:
4.4 g	**2.2 g**	**2.2 g**	**5.8 g**	**22.9 g**	**231 kcal**	**Carbs (4%)** **Protein (9%)** **Fat (87%)**

Note: Nutritional facts are calculated using Homemade Dark Chocolate made with coconut oil (see recipe on page 32).

Cinnamon Sun Squares

These nut-free fat bombs look as good as they taste: a healthy dose of turmeric turns the white chocolate topping a bright, sunshiny yellow color.

Ingredients

For the squares:

1 recipe (280 g/9.9 oz) Pumpkin Sun Butter (page 31)

⅓ cup (50 g/1.8 oz) powdered erythritol or Swerve

¼ cup (55 g/1.9 oz) coconut oil

Few drops liquid stevia, to taste (optional)

For the topping:

4.2 ounces (120 g) Homemade White Chocolate (page 34)

2 tablespoons (30 g/1.1 oz) coconut oil

¼ to ½ teaspoon turmeric powder

Instructions

To make the squares: In a food processor, combine the Pumpkin Sun Butter, erythritol or Swerve, and coconut oil. Pulse until smooth. If you want a sweeter taste, add the stevia and pulse again.

Transfer the mixture to an 8 x 8-inch (20 x 20 cm) parchment-lined pan, or a silicone pan. With a spatula, spread it over the bottom of the pan. Refrigerate for about 30 minutes, or until hardened.

To make the topping: Melt the white chocolate and coconut oil in a double boiler, or heat-proof bowl placed over a small saucepan filled with 1 cup (235 ml/8 oz) of water, over medium heat. Add the turmeric and mix until well combined. Set aside to cool.

Remove the pan from the refrigerator and pour the white chocolate on top. Refrigerate again for about 1 hour, or until set and ready to slice. Keep refrigerated for up to 1 week or freeze for up to 3 months.

Nutrition facts per serving (1 fat bomb)

| Total carbs:
4.2 g | Fiber:
1.6 g | Net carbs:
2.7 g | Protein:
4.1 g | Fat:
19.2 g | Energy:
196 kcal | Calories from:
Carbs (5%)
Protein (8%)
Fat (87%) |

Yield:
12 fat bombs

Hands-on time:
10 mins

Overall time:
**15 mins +
chilling time**

Salted Almond and Coconut Bark

Adding a pinch of sea salt to dark chocolate works wonders to highlight flavors—
especially where almonds are involved—and this bark is no exception! You'll love the way
the sea salt enhances the chocolate's deep, seductive flavors.

Ingredients

½ cup (75 g/2.6 oz) almonds

½ cup (30 g/1.1 oz)
unsweetened flaked coconut

3.5 ounces (100 g) Homemade
Dark Chocolate (page 32)

½ cup (125 g/4.4 oz) coconut
butter

½ to 1 teaspoon sugar-free
almond extract (optional)

Few drops liquid stevia, to taste
(optional)

¼ teaspoon sea salt

Instructions

Preheat the oven to 350°F (175°C, or gas mark 4).
Spread the almonds and coconut on a baking sheet.
Place it in the preheated oven and toast for 5 to 8
minutes, or until lightly golden. Stir once or twice to
prevent burning. Remove from the oven and set aside.

Melt the dark chocolate and coconut butter in a
double boiler, or heat-proof bowl placed over a small
saucepan filled with 1 cup (235 ml/8 oz) of water,
over medium heat. Add the almond extract and
stevia (if using). Mix until well combined and set
aside to cool slightly.

Pour the chocolate mixture onto a medium plate
lined with parchment paper. Scatter the toasted
coconut flakes and almonds over the top. Sprinkle
with the sea salt. Refrigerate for about 1 hour, or until
set and ready to slice. Keep refrigerated for up to 1
week or freeze for up to 3 months.

Nutrition facts per serving (1 fat bomb)

Total carbs:	Fiber:	Net carbs:	Protein:	Fat:	Energy:	Calories from:
5 g	**3.2 g**	**1.9 g**	**2.6 g**	**15.3 g**	**161 kcal**	**Carbs (5%)** **Protein (6%)** **Fat (89%)**

Note: Nutritional facts are calculated using Homemade Dark Chocolate made with unsweetened chocolate (see recipe on page 32).

Candied Bacon and Pecan Bark

Reach for one of these too-good-to-be-true fat bombs when you're craving something that's both sweet and savory.

Ingredients

6 bacon slices (180 g/6.3 oz)

2 tablespoons (28 g/1 oz) unsalted butter or coconut oil, at room temperature

¼ cup (50 g/1.8 oz) granulated erythritol or Swerve

1 cup (100 g/3.5 oz) pecans

1 teaspoon natural maple extract

Few drops liquid stevia, to taste (optional)

8.8 ounces (250 g) Homemade Dark Chocolate (page 32)

Instructions

Preheat the oven to 325°F (160°C, or gas mark 3). Line a baking sheet with parchment paper. Lay the bacon strips flat on the parchment, leaving enough space between so they don't overlap. Place the sheet in the preheated oven and cook for 25 to 30 minutes, or until golden brown. The exact amount of time depends on the thickness of the bacon slices. Remove from the oven and set aside to cool. Once cool, crumble the bacon into small bits. Pour the bacon grease into a glass container and reserve for another use—bacon grease is great for frying eggs, for instance.

In a medium saucepan set over medium heat, combine the butter or oil and erythritol or Swerve. Cook until it starts to bubble. Stir in the pecans and maple extract. Cook for about 10 minutes, or until fragrant, stirring frequently to prevent burning. Remove from the heat. If you want a sweeter taste, add the stevia and mix again.

Nutrition facts per serving (1 fat bomb)

Total carbs:	Fiber:	Net carbs:	Protein:	Fat:	Energy:	Calories from:
2.7 g	**1.4 g**	**1.3 g**	**3.2 g**	**15.6 g**	**161 kcal**	**Carbs (3%)** **Protein (8%)** **Fat (89%)**

Note: Nutritional facts are calculated using Homemade Dark Chocolate made with unsweetened chocolate (see recipe on page 32).

Yield:
16 fat bombs

Hands-on time:
15 mins

Overall time:
**40 mins +
chilling time**

Add the crumbled bacon and mix well. Spread the mixture over the surface of an 8 x 8-inch (20 x 20 cm) parchment-lined pan, or a silicone pan.

Melt the dark chocolate in a double boiler, or heat-proof bowl placed over a small saucepan filled with 1 cup (235 ml/ 8 oz) of water, over medium heat. Pour the melted chocolate over the caramelized nut mixture and set aside to cool.

When cool, refrigerate for about 1 hour, or until set and ready to slice. Keep refrigerated for up to 1 week or freeze for up to 3 months.

Yield:
16 fat bombs

Hands-on time:
10 mins

Overall time:
15 mins + chilling time

White Chocolate and Raspberry Bark

Add a little bite to your bark by strewing sweet-and-sour raspberries and crunchy nuts over a smooth white chocolate base. Fresh lemon zest peps it up even more.

Ingredients

½ cup (75 g/2.6 oz) almonds

8.8 ounces (250 g) Homemade White Chocolate (page 34)

⅓ cup (73 g/2.6 oz) coconut oil

1 to 2 teaspoons freshly grated lemon zest (optional)

Few drops liquid stevia, to taste (optional)

1 cup (150 g/5.3 oz) raspberries, frozen

Instructions

Preheat the oven to 350°F (175°C, or gas mark 4). Spread the almonds on a baking sheet. Place it in the preheated oven and toast for 5 or 8 minutes, or until lightly golden. Stir once or twice to prevent burning. Remove from the oven and set aside.

Melt the white chocolate and coconut oil in a double boiler, or heat-proof bowl placed over a small saucepan filled with 1 cup (235 ml/8 oz) of water, over medium heat. Add the lemon zest and stevia (if using). Mix until well combined and set aside to cool.

Pour the mixture into an 8 x 8-inch (20 x 20 cm) parchment-lined pan, or a silicone pan. Top with the toasted almonds and raspberries. Refrigerate for about 1 hour, or until set and ready to slice. Keep refrigerated for up to 1 week or freeze for up to 3 months.

Nutrition facts per serving (1 fat bomb)

Total carbs:	Fiber:	Net carbs:	Protein:	Fat:	Energy:	Calories from:
3.2 g	**0.9 g**	**2.3 g**	**1.5 g**	**18 g**	**175 kcal**	**Carbs (5%)** **Protein (4%)** **Fat (91%)**

Yield:	Hands-on time:	Overall time:
16 fat bombs	**15 mins**	**15 mins + chilling time**

Candied Orange and Nut Bark

Sweet and spicy, these fat bombs are based around caramelized nuts dosed with cinnamon, orange zest, and dark chocolate. They're ideal partners for some "me" time with a cup of coffee or tea.

Ingredients

2 tablespoons (28 g/1 oz) coconut oil or unsalted butter, at room temperature

¼ cup (50 g/1.8 oz) granulated erythritol or Swerve

1 tablespoon (6 g/0.2 oz) freshly grated orange zest, plus more for garnish (optional)

1 teaspoon ground cinnamon

1 cup (100 g/3.5 oz) walnuts or pecans, roughly chopped

1 cup (150 g/5.3 oz) almonds, roughly chopped

Pinch salt

Few drops liquid stevia, to taste (optional)

7.1 ounces (200 g) Homemade Dark Chocolate (page 32)

Instructions

In a medium saucepan set over medium heat, stir together the coconut oil or butter, erythritol or Swerve, orange zest, and cinnamon. Cook until the mixture starts to bubble. Add the walnuts or pecans, almonds, and salt. Cook for about 10 minutes more, or until fragrant. Stir frequently to prevent burning. Remove from the heat. If you want a sweeter taste, add the stevia and stir to combine. Spread the mixture into an 8 x 8-inch (20 x 20 cm) parchment-lined pan, or a silicone pan.

Melt the dark chocolate in a double boiler, or heat-proof bowl placed over a small saucepan filled with 1 cup (235 ml/8 oz) of water, over medium heat. Pour the melted chocolate over the caramelized nut mixture and set aside to cool. Sprinkle with more orange zest (if using). Refrigerate for about 1 hour, or until set and ready to slice. Keep refrigerated for up to 1 week or freeze for up to 3 months.

Nutrition facts per serving (1 fat bomb)

Total carbs:	Fiber:	Net carbs:	Protein:	Fat:	Energy:	Calories from:
4.6 g	**2.4 g**	**2.3 g**	**3.6 g**	**17.4 g**	**182 kcal**	**Carbs (5%)** **Protein (8%)** **Fat (87%)**

Note: Nutritional facts are calculated using Homemade Dark Chocolate made with unsweetened chocolate (see recipe on page 32).

Yield:
16 fat bombs

Hands-on time:
10 mins

Overall time:
15 mins + chilling time

Blueberry and Coconut Bark

My friends can't get enough of this treat! Topped with Berry Nut Butter (page 24) plus plenty of coconut, and dotted with juicy blueberries, these fat bombs make a great summertime snack.

Ingredients

1 cup coconut butter (250 g/ 8.8 oz)

¼ cup (55 g/1.9 oz) coconut oil

2 tablespoons (20 g/0.7 oz) powdered erythritol or Swerve

¼ cup (56 g/2 oz) unsalted butter or more coconut oil, at room temperature

Few drops liquid stevia, to taste (optional)

¼ cup (65 g/2.3 oz) Berry Nut Butter, at room temperature (page 24)

½ cup (75 g/2.6 oz) frozen blueberries

⅓ cup (20 g/0.7 oz) unsweetened flaked coconut, raw or toasted

Instructions

Melt the coconut butter and coconut oil in a double boiler, or heat-proof bowl placed over a small saucepan filled with 1 cup (235 ml/8 oz) of water, over medium heat. Stir in the erythritol or Swerve and butter or oil until melted. If you want a sweeter taste, add the stevia and mix again.

Pour the coconut mixture into an 8 x 8-inch (20 x 20 cm) parchment-lined pan, or a silicone pan. Drizzle the Berry Nut Butter over the top. Sprinkle with the blueberries and coconut.

Refrigerate for about 1 hour, or until set and ready to slice. Keep refrigerated for up to 3 days or freeze for up to 3 months.

Nutrition facts per serving (1 fat bomb)

Total carbs:	Fiber:	Net carbs:	Protein:	Fat:	Energy:	Calories from:
4.9 g	**3.1 g**	**1.8 g**	**1.4 g**	**18.2 g**	**178 kcal**	**Carbs (4%)** **Protein (3%)** **Fat (93%)**

Yield:
12 fat bombs

Hands-on time:
10 mins

Overall time:
15 mins + chilling time

Raspberry, Chocolate, and Coconut Bark

This fruity nutty bark has personality. Chocolate forms the backdrop for a mélange of macadamia nuts, raspberries, and coconut flakes—and it's all sugar-free.

Tip

If you can find them, try this recipe with blackberries. They are just as delicious as raspberries.

Ingredients

⅓ cup (20 g/0.7 oz) unsweetened flaked coconut

½ cup (65 g/2.3 oz) macadamia nuts

1 cup (250 g/8.8 oz) coconut butter

¼ cup (55 g/1.9 oz) coconut oil

¼ cup (56 g/2 oz) unsalted butter or more coconut oil, at room temperature

⅓ cup (30 g/1 oz) unsweetened cacao powder

¼ cup (40 g/4.1 oz) powdered erythritol or Swerve

Few drops liquid stevia, to taste (optional)

½ cup (75 g/2.6 oz) frozen raspberries (see Tip)

Pinch sea salt

Instructions

Preheat the oven to 350°F (175°C, or gas mark 4). Spread the coconut and macadamia nuts on a baking sheet. Place it in the preheated oven and toast for 5 to 8 minutes, or until lightly golden. Stir once or twice to prevent burning. Remove from the oven and set aside.

Melt the coconut butter and coconut oil in a double boiler, or heat-proof bowl placed over a small saucepan filled with 1 cup (235 ml/8 oz) of water, over medium heat. Stir in the butter or oil until melted. Remove from the heat. Add the cacao powder and erythritol or Swerve and mix until well combined. If you want a sweeter taste, add the stevia and mix again.

Pour the chocolate-coconut mixture onto a medium plate or tray lined with parchment paper. Scatter the raspberries, toasted macadamia nuts, and coconut over the chocolate. Sprinkle with the sea salt.

Refrigerate for about 1 hour, or until set and ready to slice. Keep refrigerated for up to 3 days or freeze for up to 3 months.

Nutrition facts per serving (1 fat bomb)

Total carbs:	Fiber:	Net carbs:	Protein:	Fat:	Energy:	Calories from:
7.6 g	**14.8 g**	**2.7 g**	**2.4 g**	**25.4 g**	**248 kcal**	**Carbs (4%)** **Protein (4%)** **Fat (92%)**

Fat-Burning Keto Bark

Thanks to the MCTs (medium-chain triglycerides) in the coconut oil, this crunchy, chocolaty bark works overtime when it comes to promoting fat loss. It'll help you feel fuller longer, and will satisfy stubborn sweet cravings, too.

Ingredients

⅔ cup (145 g/5.1 oz) cacao butter

2 tablespoons (28 g/1 oz) coconut oil

⅓ cup (85 g/3 oz) Almond and Cashew Butter (page 16) or almond butter

2 teaspoons sugar-free vanilla extract or 1 teaspoon vanilla powder, or ground cinnamon

2 tablespoons (20 g/0.7 oz) powdered erythritol or Swerve

¼ cup (30 g/1.1 oz) coconut milk powder or 2 tablespoons (32 g/1.1 oz) coconut butter

Few drops liquid stevia, to taste (optional)

¼ cup (30 g/1.1 oz) cacao nibs or extra-dark chocolate chips, 90 percent cacao or more

Instructions

Melt the cacao butter and coconut oil in a double boiler, or heat-proof bowl placed over a small saucepan filled with 1 cup (235 ml/8 oz) of water, over medium heat. Add the nut butter, vanilla or cinnamon, erythritol or Swerve, and coconut milk powder or coconut butter. Mix until well combined. If you want a sweeter taste, add the stevia and mix again.

Pour the mixture onto a medium plate lined with parchment paper. Top with the cacao nibs or chocolate chips.

Refrigerate for about 1 hour, or until set and ready to slice. Keep refrigerated for up to 1 week or freeze for up to 3 months.

Nutrition facts per serving (1 fat bomb)

Total carbs:	Fiber:	Net carbs:	Protein:	Fat:	Energy:	Calories from:
2.8 g	**0.8 g**	**1.9 g**	**1.7 g**	**21.5 g**	**205 kcal**	**Carbs (4%)** **Protein (3%)** **Fat (93%)**

Yield:
12 fat bombs

Hands-on time:
15 mins

Overall time:
15 mins + chilling time

Chapter 4

Frozen Fat Bombs

If ice cream is one of your favorite indulgences, you're in luck! (Yes, even on a low-carb eating plan.) That's because the bite-size frozen fat bombs in this chapter are its close cousin: they're sweet, lush, and laden with goodies like fruit, chocolate, and coconut. There are even a couple recipes for homemade ice cream you can enjoy by the scoop! If you like to keep things simple, you'll love the recipes for fat bombs with classic flavors, like my Strawberry Cheesecake Ice Bombs (page 106), or the Vanilla Ice Bombs (page 124). If you're a bit more adventurous, try the Strawberry-Basil Ice Cups (page 113) or the Pumpkin Pie Ice Bombs (page 111). All of these fat bombs keep for up to 3 months in the freezer, so you'll never be without a quick, crave-busting, healthy, low-carb snack again.

Yield:
10 ice bombs

Hands-on time:
15 mins

Overall time:
**15 mins +
freezing time**

Strawberry Cheesecake Ice Bombs

These fat bombs—the most popular I've ever created—went viral over social media! And that's probably because they have all the fruity creaminess of real strawberry cheesecake.

Ingredients

½ cup (70 g/2.5 oz) strawberries, fresh, or frozen and thawed

⅔ cup (160 g/5.6 oz) full-fat cream cheese or creamed coconut milk

¼ cup (56 g/2 oz) unsalted butter or coconut oil, at room temperature

2 tablespoons (20 g/0.7 oz) powdered erythritol or Swerve

1 teaspoon sugar-free vanilla extract or ½ teaspoon vanilla powder

Few drops liquid stevia, to taste (optional)

Instructions

If using creamed coconut milk, make it following the instructions on page 10.

In a food processor, combine the strawberries, cream cheese or creamed coconut milk, butter or coconut oil, erythritol or Swerve, and vanilla. Pulse until smooth and creamy. If you want a sweeter taste, add the stevia and pulse again. Spoon about 2 tablespoons (30 g/1.1 oz) of the mixture into each of 10 small silicone muffin molds or candy molds, or use round cake pop molds for a round bomb shape. Freeze for about 2 hours, or until set. Keep frozen for up to 3 months.

Nutrition facts per serving (1 ice bomb)

Total carbs:	Fiber:	Net carbs:	Protein:	Fat:	Energy:	Calories from:
1.2 g	**0.2 g**	**1.1 g**	**1.1 g**	**9.1 g**	**83 kcal**	**Carbs (5%)** **Protein (5%)** **Fat (90%)**

Sweet and Savory Fat Bombs

Yield:
10 ice bombs

Hands-on time:
15 mins

Overall time:
**15 mins +
freezing time**

Lemon and Lime Cheesecake Ice Bombs

If you're on a fat fast this summer, keep a batch of these citrusy fat bombs waiting in the freezer; they're great for warm-weather snacking.

Ingredients

1 cup (240 g/8.5 oz) full-fat cream cheese or creamed coconut milk

¼ cup (56 g/2 oz) unsalted butter or coconut oil, at room temperature

2 tablespoons (20 g/0.7 oz) powdered erythritol or Swerve

1 tablespoon (15 ml/0.5 fl oz) freshly squeezed lemon juice or lime juice

2 teaspoons freshly grated lemon zest or lime zest

Few drops liquid stevia, to taste (optional)

Instructions

If using creamed coconut milk, make it following the instructions on page 10.

In a food processor or with a mixer, combine the cream cheese or creamed coconut milk, butter or coconut oil, erythritol or Swerve, lemon or lime juice, and lemon zest. Pulse until smooth and creamy. If you want a sweeter taste, add the stevia and pulse again.

Spoon about 2 tablespoons (30 g/1.1 oz) of the mixture into each of 10 small silicone muffin molds or candy molds, or use round cake pop molds for a round bomb shape. Freeze for about 2 hours, or until set. Keep frozen for up to 3 months.

Nutrition facts per serving (1 ice bomb)

Total carbs:	Fiber:	Net carbs:	Protein:	Fat:	Energy:	Calories from:
1.1 g	**0.1 g**	**1 g**	**1.7 g**	**11.3 g**	**100 kcal**	**Carbs (3%)** **Protein (6%)** **Fat (91%)**

| Yield: **14 ice bombs** | Hands-on time: **15 mins** | Overall time: **15 mins + freezing time** |

Mint and Chocolate Chip Ice Bombs

Packed with healthy fats—and loaded with potassium and B vitamins—avocado lends these frozen mint-chocolate fat bombs an incredibly silky texture.

Ingredients

1 medium (150 g/5.3 oz) ripe avocado, halved, pitted, and peeled

1 cup (240 g/8.5 oz) full-fat mascarpone cheese or creamed coconut milk

¼ cup plus 1 tablespoon (50 g/ 1.8 oz) powdered erythritol or Swerve

1 teaspoon peppermint extract, or 1 tablespoon (6 g/0.2 oz) fresh mint

Few drops liquid stevia, to taste (optional)

2.1 ounces (60 g) Homemade Dark Chocolate (page 32), chopped

Instructions

If using creamed coconut milk, make it following the instructions on page 10.

In a food processor or with a mixer, combine the avocado flesh, mascarpone or creamed coconut milk, erythritol or Swerve, and mint extract or fresh mint. If you want a sweeter taste, add the stevia. Pulse until smooth. Mix in the chopped dark chocolate.

Spoon about 2 tablespoons (35 g/1.2 oz) of the mixture into each of 14 small silicone muffin molds or candy molds, or use round cake pop molds for a round bomb shape. Freeze for about 2 hours, or until set. Keep frozen for up to 3 months.

Nutrition facts per serving (1 ice bomb)

| Total carbs: **2.7 g** | Fiber: **1.2 g** | Net carbs: **1.5 g** | Protein: **1.6 g** | Fat: **9.5 g** | Energy: **100 kcal** | Calories from: **Carbs (6%)** **Protein (7%)** **Fat (87%)** |

Note: Nutritional facts are calculated using Homemade Dark Chocolate made with unsweetened chocolate (see recipe on page 32).

Yield:	Hands-on time:	Overall time:
10 ice bombs	**15 mins**	**15 mins + freezing time**

Pumpkin Pie Ice Bombs

Pumpkin pie isn't just for Thanksgiving! These frozen, bite-size versions of the popular holiday dessert make a delicious year-round snack.

Ingredients

1 cup (240 g/8.5 oz) full-fat mascarpone cheese or creamed coconut milk

¼ cup (50 g/1.8 oz) unsweetened pumpkin puree

2 tablespoons (20 g/0.7 oz) powdered erythritol or Swerve

1 teaspoon pumpkin pie spice mix

Few drops liquid stevia, to taste (optional)

Instructions

If using creamed coconut milk, make it following the instructions on page 10.

In a food processor, combine the mascarpone or creamed coconut milk, pumpkin purée, erythritol or Swerve, and pumpkin pie spice mix. Pulse until smooth and creamy. If you want a sweeter taste, add the stevia and pulse again.

Spoon about 2 tablespoons (30 g/1.1 oz) of the mixture into each of 10 small silicone muffin molds or candy molds, or use round cake pop molds for a round bomb shape. Freeze for about 2 hours, or until set. Keep frozen for up to 3 months.

Nutrition facts per serving (1 ice bomb)

Total carbs:	Fiber:	Net carbs:	Protein:	Fat:	Energy:	Calories from:
1.1 g	**0.2 g**	**0.9 g**	**1.4 g**	**8.5 g**	**87 kcal**	**Carbs (4%)** **Protein (7%)** **Fat (89%)**

Yield:
10 ice cups

Hands-on time:
15 mins

Overall time:
15 mins + freezing time

Strawberry-Basil Ice Cups

Summery, spicy, and fragrant, fresh basil is a wonderful foil for the candied sweetness of strawberries in these frosty fat bombs. If the strawberry-basil combination sounds odd to you, just try it once: it'll win you over I'm sure!

Ingredients

½ cup (120 g/4.2 oz) creamed coconut milk, at room temperature

¾ cup (180 g/6.3 oz) cream cheese or more creamed coconut milk, at room temperature

¼ cup (40 g/4.9 oz) powdered erythritol or Swerve

¼ cup (56 g/2 oz) unsalted butter or coconut oil, at room temperature

1 teaspoon sugar-free vanilla extract, or ½ teaspoon vanilla powder

Few drops liquid stevia, to taste (optional)

1 cup (140 g/5 oz) fresh strawberries

2 tablespoons (5 g/0.2 oz) fresh basil leaves

Instructions

To make creamed coconut milk, follow the instructions on page 10.

In a food processor, combine the creamed coconut milk, cream cheese or more creamed coconut milk, erythritol or Swerve, butter or coconut oil, and vanilla. Pulse until smooth and creamy. If you want a sweeter taste, add the stevia and pulse again.

Remove half of the mixture from the processor and set aside. To the remaining mixture in the processor, add about ¾ cup (105 g/3.8 oz) of strawberries. Pulse until smooth. Slice the remaining ¼ cup of strawberries and reserve for topping.

Divide the strawberry cream cheese mixture among 10 silicone muffin cups.

In a clean food processor, combine the other half of the cream cheese with the basil. Pulse until smooth. Top each cup with 1½ tablespoons (20 g/0.7 oz) of the basil mixture and finish each with a few strawberry slices. Freeze for about 2 hours, or until set. Keep frozen for up to 3 months.

Nutrition facts per serving (1 ice cup)

Total carbs:	Fiber:	Net carbs:	Protein:	Fat:	Energy:	Calories from:
2.8 g	**0.6 g**	**2.2 g**	**2 g**	**13.9 g**	**131 kcal**	**Carbs (6%)** **Protein (5%)** **Fat (89%)**

Vanilla-Keto Ice Cream

This low-carb ice cream is a scoopable fat bomb—and it's so ridiculously rich and creamy that you'll mistake it for frozen vanilla custard.

Ingredients

1½ cups (360 g/12.7 oz) creamed coconut milk

6 large egg yolks

2 large eggs

¼ cup (40 g/1.4 oz) powdered erythritol or Swerve

¼ cup (60 ml/2 fl oz) MCT oil

2 teaspoons sugar-free vanilla extract or 1 teaspoon vanilla powder

Few drops liquid stevia, to taste (optional)

Instructions

To make creamed coconut milk, follow the instructions on page 10.

In a food processor, combine the creamed coconut milk, egg yolks, eggs, erythritol or Swerve, MCT oil, and vanilla. Pulse until smooth and creamy. If you want a sweeter taste, add the stevia and pulse again.

Pour the mixture into an ice cream maker and process according to the manufacturer's instructions. Once the ice cream is churned, freeze for about 30 minutes before serving. Keep frozen for up to 3 months.

Nutrition facts per serving (1 scoop [⅓ cup/85 g/3 oz])

Total carbs:	Fiber:	Net carbs:	Protein:	Fat:	Energy:	Calories from:
3.9 g	**1 g**	**2.9 g**	**5.2 g**	**27.1 g**	**270 kcal**	**Carbs (4%)** **Protein (8%)** **Fat (88%)**

Yield:
**8 servings/
scoops**

Hands-on time:
10 mins

Overall time:
**45 mins +
freezing time**

Worried about using raw eggs?
It's easy to make raw eggs safe for
consumption by pasteurizing them, and
it only takes a few minutes. Learn how on
page 12.

Decadent Chocolate-Keto Ice Cream

You're eating low-carb, but that doesn't mean you can't indulge in chocolate ice cream now and again! This keto-friendly dark chocolate version is so captivating, it'll make you weak in the knees.

Ingredients

1 large (200 g/7.1 oz) ripe avocado, halved, pitted, and peeled

1½ cups (360 g/12.7 oz) creamed coconut milk

½ cup (40 g/1.4 oz) unsweetened cacao powder

⅓ cup (50 g/1.8 oz) powdered erythritol or Swerve

¼ cup (60 ml/2 fl oz) MCT oil

Pinch salt

Few drops liquid stevia, to taste (optional)

Instructions

To make creamed coconut milk, follow the instructions on page 10.

In a food processor, combine the avocado flesh, creamed coconut milk, cacao powder, erythritol or Swerve, MCT oil, and salt. Pulse until smooth and creamy. If you want a sweeter taste, add the stevia and pulse again.

Pour the mixture into an ice cream maker and process according to the manufacturer's instructions. Once the ice cream is churned, freeze for about 30 minutes before serving. Keep frozen for up to 3 months.

Nutrition facts per serving (1 scoop [⅓ cup/85 g/3 oz])

Total carbs:	Fiber:	Net carbs:	Protein:	Fat:	Energy:	Calories from:
8.3 g	**4.3 g**	**4 g**	**3.1 g**	**26.8 g**	**260 kcal**	**Carbs (6%)** **Protein (5%)** **Fat (89%)**

Yield:
8 servings/ scoops

Hands-on time:
10 mins

Overall time:
45 mins + freezing time

Tiramisu Ice Bombs

Tiramisu **means "pick me up" in Italian, and these dark chocolate–coated frozen fat bombs do just that: they'll boost your energy (and your mood, too, if you love tiramisu as much as I do!). Laced with coffee and rum flavorings, they're every bit as good as the original.**

Ingredients

For the ice bombs:

1¼ cups (300 g/10.6 oz) full-fat mascarpone cheese or creamed coconut milk

¼ cup (40 g/1.4 oz) powdered erythritol or Swerve

1 to 2 teaspoons sugar-free rum extract

¼ cup (60 ml/2 fl oz) strong brewed coffee, chilled (see Tip)

Few drops liquid stevia, to taste (optional)

For the coating (or use any of the Homemade Dark Chocolate recipes [page 32]):

2.5 ounces (70 g) extra-dark 90 percent chocolate

1 ounce (28 g) cacao butter

Instructions

If using creamed coconut milk, make it following the instructions on page 10.

To make the ice bombs: In a food processor or with a mixer, combine the mascarpone or creamed coconut milk, erythritol or Swerve, rum extract, and chilled coffee. Pulse until smooth and creamy. If you want a sweeter taste, add the stevia and pulse again.

Spoon about 2 tablespoons (35 g/ 1.2 oz) of the mixture into each of 12 small silicone muffin molds or candy molds, or use round cake pop molds for a round bomb shape. Freeze for about 2 hours, or until set.

To make the coating: Melt the dark chocolate and cacao butter in a double boiler, or heat-proof bowl placed over a small saucepan filled with 1 cup (235 ml/ 8 oz) of water, over medium heat. Mix well. Cool the mixture before use. It should not be hot, but should still be liquid. If you are using any of the Homemade Dark Chocolate recipes on page 32, you may need as much as 4.6 to 4.9 ounces (130 to 140 g) to coat all the ice bombs.

Nutrition facts per serving (1 ice bomb)

Total carbs:	Fiber:	Net carbs:	Protein:	Fat:	Energy:	Calories from:
1.8 g	**0.4 g**	**1.4 g**	**2 g**	**14.5 g**	**143 kcal**	**Carbs (4%)** **Protein (6%)** **Fat (90%)**

Yield:
12 ice bombs

Hands-on time:
20 mins

Overall time:
**30 mins +
freezing time**

Work in batches of 3 or 4 to prevent the ice bombs from melting. Gently pierce each frozen ice bomb with a toothpick or a fork. One at a time, hold the ice bomb over the melted chocolate and spoon the chocolate over it to coat completely. Turn the stick as you work until the coating is solidified. Place the coated ice bombs on a parchment-lined tray.

Freeze the coated pieces, in batches as you work, for at least 15 minutes to harden. Keep frozen for up to 3 months.

Tip
For a naturally caffeine-free alternative to regular coffee, try 1 to 2 teaspoons of caffeine-free instant coffee powder made from chicory root or dandelion instead.

Chocolate-Covered Coconut Ice Bombs

These are my favorite frozen fat bombs: they're like bite-size coconut cream pies that have been dunked in dark chocolate. Even better, they're surprisingly simple—all you need is a few basic ingredients.

Ingredients

For the ice bombs:

1½ cups (360 g/12.7 oz) creamed coconut milk

¼ cup (40 g/1.4 oz) powdered erythritol or Swerve

1 teaspoon sugar-free vanilla extract or ½ teaspoon vanilla powder

Few drops liquid stevia, to taste (optional)

For the coating (or use any of the Homemade Dark Chocolate recipes [page 32]):

2.5 ounces (70 g) extra-dark 90 percent chocolate

1 ounce (28 g) cacao butter

½ cup (35 g/1.2 oz) unsweetened shredded coconut

Instructions

To make creamed coconut milk, follow the instructions on page 10.

To make the ice bombs: In a food processor or with a mixer, combine the creamed coconut milk, erythritol or Swerve, and vanilla. Pulse until smooth and creamy. If you want a sweeter taste, add the stevia and pulse again.

Spoon about 2 tablespoons (35 g/ 1.2 oz) of the mixture into each of 12 small silicone muffin molds or candy molds, or use round cake pop molds for a round bomb shape. Freeze for about 2 hours, or until set.

To make the coating: Melt the dark chocolate and cacao butter in a double boiler, or heat-proof bowl placed over a small saucepan filled with 1 cup (235 ml/ 8 oz) of water, over medium heat. Mix well. Cool before you use. It should not be hot, but should still be liquid. If you are using any of the Homemade Dark Chocolate recipes on page 32, you may need as much as 4.6 to 4.9 ounces (130 to 140 g) to coat all the ice bombs.

Nutrition facts per serving (1 ice bomb)

Total carbs:	Fiber:	Net carbs:	Protein:	Fat:	Energy:	Calories from:
4 g	**1.5 g**	**2.5 g**	**2.3 g**	**16.4 g**	**163 kcal**	**Carbs (6%)** **Protein (5%)** **Fat (89%)**

Yield:
12 ice bombs

Hands-on time:
20 mins

Overall time:
**30 mins +
freezing time**

Preheat the oven to 350°F (175°C, or gas mark 4). Spread the coconut on a baking sheet. Place it in the preheated oven and toast for 5 to 8 minutes, or until lightly golden. Stir once or twice to prevent burning. Remove from the oven and set aside.

Work in batches of 3 or 4 to prevent the ice bombs from melting. Gently pierce each frozen ice bomb with a toothpick or a fork. One at a time, hold each ice bomb over the melted chocolate and spoon the chocolate over it to coat completely. Turn the stick as you work until the coating is solidified. Place the coated ice bombs on a parchment-lined tray. Before they become completely solid, roll them in the toasted coconut.

Freeze the coated pieces, in batches as you work, for at least 15 minutes to harden. Keep frozen for up to 3 months.

Dark Chocolate and Cherry Ice Bombs

These ice bombs are a low-carb take on that box of chocolate-covered cherries your grandmother kept on her kitchen counter. It's a timeless match, too: the almond-scented fruitiness of cherry is at its best when it's draped with dark chocolate.

Ingredients

For the ice bombs:

1 cup (240 g/8.5 oz) full-fat mascarpone cheese or creamed coconut milk

¾ cup (110 g/3.9 oz) cherries, pitted and frozen

2 tablespoons (20 g/0.7 oz) powdered erythritol or Swerve

1 teaspoon sugar-free vanilla extract or ½ teaspoon vanilla powder

1 to 2 teaspoons sugar-free cherry extract

Few drops liquid stevia, to taste (optional)

For the coating (or use any of the Homemade Dark Chocolate recipes [page 32]):

2.5 ounces (70 g) extra-dark 90 percent chocolate

1 ounce (28 g) cacao butter

Instructions

If using creamed coconut milk, make it following the instructions on page 10.

To make the ice bombs: In a food processor, combine the mascarpone or creamed coconut milk, cherries, erythritol or Swerve, vanilla, and cherry extract. Pulse until smooth and creamy. If you want a sweeter taste, add the stevia and pulse again.

The cherries in this mixture make it softer than other recipes: use molds deep enough so the mixture doesn't leak out. Spoon about 2 tablespoons (30 g/1.1 oz) of the mixture into each of 12 silicone muffin molds or candy molds, or use round cake pop molds for a round bomb shape. Freeze for about 2 hours, or until set.

To make the coating: Melt the dark chocolate and cacao butter in a double boiler, or heat-proof bowl placed over a small saucepan filled with 1 cup (235 ml/ 8 oz) of water, over medium heat. Mix well. Cool before use. It should not be hot, but should still be liquid. If you are using any of the Homemade Dark Chocolate recipes on page 32, you may need as much as 4.6 to 4.9 ounces (130 to 140 g) to coat all the ice bombs.

Nutrition facts per serving (1 ice bomb)

Total carbs:	Fiber:	Net carbs:	Protein:	Fat:	Energy:	Calories from:
2.7 g	**0.6 g**	**2.1 g**	**1.8 g**	**12.4 g**	**131 kcal**	**Carbs (6%)** **Protein (6%)** **Fat (88%)**

Yield:
12 ice bombs

Hands-on time:
20 mins

Overall time:
**30 mins +
freezing time**

Work in batches of 3 or 4 to prevent the ice bombs from melting. Gently pierce each frozen ice bomb with a toothpick or a fork. One at a time, hold the ice bomb over the melted chocolate and spoon the chocolate over it to coat completely. Turn the stick as you work until the coating is solidified. Place the coated ice bombs on a parchment-lined tray.

Freeze the coated pieces, in batches as you work, for at least 15 minutes to harden. Keep frozen for up to 3 months.

Vanilla Ice Bombs

Elaborate toppings and unusual flavor combinations are lots of fun, but for purists at heart, it's hard to beat the simple, elegant combination of chocolate-coated vanilla ice cream—the inspiration behind these fabulous low-carb ice bombs.

Ingredients

For the ice bombs:

1 cup (240 g/8.5 oz) full-fat mascarpone cheese or creamed coconut milk

¼ cup (40 g/1.4 oz) powdered erythritol or Swerve

¼ cup (60 ml/2 fl oz) heavy whipping cream or coconut milk

2 teaspoons sugar-free vanilla extract or 1 teaspoon vanilla powder

Few drops liquid stevia, to taste (optional)

For the coating (or use any of the Homemade Dark Chocolate recipes [page 32]):

2.5 ounces (70 g) extra-dark 90 percent chocolate

1 ounce (28 g) cacao butter

Instructions

If using creamed coconut milk, make it following the instructions on page 10.

To make the ice bombs: In a food processor, combine the mascarpone or creamed coconut milk, erythritol or Swerve, cream or coconut milk, and vanilla. Pulse until smooth and creamy. If you want a sweeter taste, add the stevia and pulse again.

Spoon about 2 tablespoons (30 g/ 1.1 oz) of the mixture into each of 12 small silicone muffin molds or candy molds, or use round cake pop molds for a round bomb shape. Freeze for about 2 hours, or until set.

To make the coating: Melt the dark chocolate and cacao butter in a double boiler, or heat-proof bowl placed over a small saucepan filled with 1 cup (235 ml/ 8 oz) of water, over medium heat. Mix well. Cool the mixture before use. It should not be hot, but should still be liquid. If you are using any of the Homemade Dark Chocolate recipes on page 32, you may need as much as 4.6 to 4.9 ounces (130 to 140 g) to coat all the ice bombs.

Nutrition facts per serving (1 ice bomb)

Total carbs:	Fiber:	Net carbs:	Protein:	Fat:	Energy:	Calories from:
1.9 g	**0.4 g**	**1.5 g**	**1.8 g**	**14.6 g**	**144 kcal**	**Carbs (4%)** **Protein (5%)** **Fat (91%)**

Work in batches of 3 or 4 to prevent the ice bombs from melting. Gently pierce each frozen ice bomb with a toothpick or a fork. One at a time, hold each ice bomb over the melted chocolate and spoon the chocolate over it to coat completely. Turn the stick as you work until the coating is solidified. Place the coated ice bombs on a parchment-lined tray.

Freeze the coated pieces, in batches as you work, for at least 15 minutes to harden. Keep frozen for up to 3 months.

Mocha Ice Bombs

Being a serious coffee lover, I'm a huge fan of these creamy fat bombs, in which sweetened mascarpone cheese is dosed with coffee and chocolate before being swathed in— you guessed it—even more rich dark chocolate.

Ingredients

For the ice bombs:

1 cup (240 g/8.5 oz) full-fat mascarpone cheese or creamed coconut milk

¼ cup (40 g/1.4 oz) powdered erythritol or Swerve

2 tablespoons (10 g/0.4 oz) unsweetened cacao powder

¼ cup (60 ml/2 fl oz) strong brewed coffee, chilled

Few drops liquid stevia, to taste (optional)

For the coating (or use any of the Homemade Dark Chocolate recipes [page 32]):

2.5 ounces (70 g) extra-dark 90 percent chocolate

1 ounce (28 g) cacao butter

Instructions

If using creamed coconut milk, make it following the instructions on page 10.

To make the ice bombs: In a food processor or with a mixer, combine the mascarpone or creamed coconut milk, erythritol or Swerve, cacao powder, and coffee. Pulse until smooth and creamy. If you want a sweeter taste, add the stevia and pulse again.

Spoon about 2 tablespoons (30 g/ 1.1 oz) of the mixture into each of 12 small silicone muffin molds or candy molds, or use round cake pop molds for a round bomb shape. Freeze for about 2 hours, or until set.

To make the coating: Melt the dark chocolate and cacao butter in a double boiler, or heat-proof bowl placed over a small saucepan filled with 1 cup (235 ml/ 8 oz) of water, over medium heat. Mix well. Cool the mixture before use. It should not be hot, but should still be liquid. If you are using any of the Homemade Dark Chocolate recipes on page 32, you may need as much as 4.6 to 4.9 ounces (130 to 140 g) to coat all the ice bombs.

Nutrition facts per serving (1 ice bomb)

Total carbs:	Fiber:	Net carbs:	Protein:	Fat:	Energy:	Calories from:
2.2 g	**0.7 g**	**1.5 g**	**1.9 g**	**12.9 g**	**127 kcal**	**Carbs (5%)** **Protein (6%)** **Fat (89%)**

Yield:
12 ice bombs

Hands-on time:
20 mins

Overall time:
**30 mins +
freezing time**

Work in batches of 3 or 4 to prevent the ice bombs from melting. Gently pierce each frozen ice bomb with a toothpick or a fork. One at a time, hold the ice bomb over the melted chocolate and spoon the chocolate over it to coat completely. Turn the stick as you work until the coating is solidified. Place the coated ice bombs on a parchment-lined tray.

Freeze the coated pieces, in batches as you work, for at least 15 minutes to harden. Keep frozen for up to 3 months.

Tip

Avoiding caffeine? As with the Tiramisu Ice Bombs (page 118), try 1 to 2 teaspoons of caffeine-free instant coffee powder made from chicory root or dandelion instead.

White Chocolate and Blueberry Ice Bombs

Blueberry is so at home encased in white chocolate, which seems to enhance the berry's floral fragrance and sweetness. Serve them up together in these frozen low-carb treats.

Ingredients

For the ice bombs:

1 cup (240 g/8.5 oz) full-fat mascarpone cheese or creamed coconut milk

¾ cup (110 g/3.9 oz) frozen blueberries

2 tablespoons (20 g/0.7 oz) powdered erythritol or Swerve

Few drops liquid stevia, to taste (optional)

For the coating:

4.2 ounces (120 g) Homemade White Chocolate (page 34)

Instructions

If using creamed coconut milk, make it following the instructions on page 10.

To make the ice bombs: In a food processor or with a mixer, combine the mascarpone or creamed coconut milk, blueberries, and erythritol or Swerve. Pulse until smooth and creamy. If you want a sweeter taste, add the stevia and pulse again.

The blueberries in this mixture make it softer than other recipes; use molds deep enough so the mixture doesn't leak out. Spoon about 2 tablespoons (30 g/1.1 oz) of the mixture into each of 12 small silicone muffin molds or candy molds, or use round cake pop molds for a round bomb shape. Freeze for about 2 hours, or until set.

To make the coating: Melt the white chocolate in a double boiler, or heat-proof bowl placed over a small saucepan filled with 1 cup (235 ml/8 oz) of water, over medium heat. Mix well. Cool the mixture before use. It should not be hot, but should still be liquid.

Nutrition facts per serving (1 ice bomb)

Total carbs:	Fiber:	Net carbs:	Protein:	Fat:	Energy:	Calories from:
2.2 g	**0.2 g**	**2 g**	**1.4 g**	**14.2 g**	**141 kcal**	**Carbs (6%)** **Protein (4%)** **Fat (90%)**

Yield:
12 ice bombs

Hands-on time:
20 mins

Overall time:
30 mins + freezing time

Work in batches of 3 or 4 to prevent the ice bombs from melting. Gently pierce each frozen ice bomb with a toothpick or a fork. One at a time, hold each ice bomb over the melted chocolate and spoon the chocolate over it to coat completely. Turn the stick as you work until the coating is solidified. Place the coated ice bombs on a parchment-lined tray.

Freeze the coated pieces, in batches as you work, for at least 15 minutes to harden. Keep frozen for up to 3 months.

Creamy Orange Ice Bombs

Bind the warm, seductive flavors of cinnamon and orange with mascarpone and cream, then ice them and coat them with coconut butter. The result? A wonderfully refreshing sugar-free snack.

Ingredients

For the ice bombs:

1 cup (240 g/8.5 oz) full-fat mascarpone cheese or creamed coconut milk

¼ cup (60 ml/2 fl oz) heavy whipping cream or coconut milk

¼ cup (40 g/1.4 oz) powdered erythritol or Swerve

1 tablespoon (6 g/0.2 oz) freshly grated orange zest or 1 to 2 teaspoons sugar-free orange extract

¼ teaspoon ground cinnamon

Few drops liquid stevia, to taste (optional)

For the coating:

⅔ cup (142 g/5 oz) coconut butter

2 tablespoons (28 g/1 oz) coconut oil

1 teaspoon freshly grated orange zest

Pinch ground cinnamon

Instructions

If using creamed coconut milk, make it following the instructions on page 10.

To make the ice bombs: In a food processor or with a mixer, combine the mascarpone or creamed coconut milk, cream or coconut milk, erythritol or Swerve, orange zest or extract, and cinnamon. Pulse until smooth and creamy. If you want a sweeter taste, add the stevia and pulse again.

Spoon about 2 tablespoons (30 g/ 1.1 oz) of the mixture into each of 12 small silicone muffin molds or candy molds, or use round cake pop molds for a round bomb shape. Freeze for about 2 hours, or until set.

To make the coating: Melt together the coconut butter, coconut oil, orange zest, and cinnamon in a double boiler, or heat-proof bowl placed over a small saucepan filled with 1 cup (235 ml/8 oz) of water, over medium heat. Cool before use. It should not be hot, but should still be liquid.

Nutrition facts per serving (1 ice bomb)

Total carbs:	Fiber:	Net carbs:	Protein:	Fat:	Energy:	Calories from:
3.4 g	**1.9 g**	**1.5 g**	**2 g**	**17.7 g**	**176 kcal**	**Carbs (3%)** **Protein (5%)** **Fat (92%)**

Yield:
12 ice bombs

Hands-on time:
20 mins

Overall time:
**30 mins +
freezing time**

Work in batches of 3 or 4 to prevent the ice bombs from melting. Gently pierce each frozen ice bomb with a toothpick or a fork. One at a time, hold each ice bomb over the coconut mixture and spoon the mixture over it to coat completely. Turn the stick as you work until the coating is solidified. Place the coated ice bombs on a parchment-lined tray and drizzle any remaining coating over them.

Freeze the coated pieces, in batches as you work, for at least 15 minutes to harden. Keep frozen for up to 3 months.

Raspberry and Lemon Ice Bombs

Like blueberries, raspberries are wonderful when they're blended with vanilla-tinged mascarpone in these keto-friendly fat bombs. Adding a little lemon to the coconut butter coating gives them just the right amount of zing.

Ingredients

For the ice bombs:

1 cup (240 g/8.5 oz) full-fat mascarpone cheese or creamed coconut milk

¾ cup (110 g/3.9 oz) frozen raspberries

3 tablespoons (20 g/0.7 oz) powdered erythritol or Swerve

1 teaspoon sugar-free vanilla extract or ½ teaspoon vanilla powder

Few drops liquid stevia, to taste (optional)

For the coating:

⅔ cup (142 g/5 oz) coconut butter

2 tablespoons (28 g/1 oz) coconut oil

1 teaspoon freshly grated lemon zest

Pinch ground cinnamon

Instructions

If using creamed coconut milk, make it following the instructions on page 10.

To make the ice bombs: In a food processor or with a mixer, combine the mascarpone or creamed coconut milk, raspberries, erythritol or Swerve, and vanilla. Pulse until smooth and creamy. If you want a sweeter taste, add the stevia and pulse again.

The raspberries in this mixture make it softer than other recipes; use molds deep enough so the mixture doesn't leak out. Spoon about 2 tablespoons (30 g/1.1 oz) of the mixture into each of 12 small silicone muffin molds or candy molds, or use round cake pop molds for a round bomb shape. Freeze for about 2 hours, or until set.

To make the coating: Melt together the coconut butter, coconut oil, lemon zest, and cinnamon in a double boiler, or heat-proof bowl placed over a small saucepan filled with 1 cup (235 ml/8 oz) of water, over medium heat. Cool before use. It should not be hot, but should still be liquid.

Nutrition facts per serving (1 ice bomb)

Total carbs:	Fiber:	Net carbs:	Protein:	Fat:	Energy:	Calories from:
3.6 g	**2.1 g**	**1.6 g**	**2 g**	**15.8 g**	**160 kcal**	**Carbs (4%)** **Protein (5%)** **Fat (91%)**

Yield:
12 ice bombs

Hands-on time:
20 mins

Overall time:
30 mins + freezing time

Work in batches of 3 or 4 to prevent the ice bombs from melting. Gently pierce each frozen ice bomb with a toothpick or a fork. One at a time, hold each ice bomb over the coconut mixture and spoon the mixture over it to coat completely. Turn the stick as you work until the coating is solidified. Place the coated ice bombs on a parchment-lined tray.

Freeze the coated pieces, in batches as you work, for at least 15 minutes to harden. Keep frozen for up to 3 months.

Chapter 5

Liquid Fat Bombs

Fat bombs don't have to be truffle-shaped. They come in lots of different shapes and sizes—including refreshing smoothies and satisfying hot beverages. And plenty of the liquid fat bombs in this chapter are nutritious enough to count as complete meals. They're all high in healthy fats, which help you stay fuller longer, so they're perfect for breakfasts or light lunches. And they're quick to prepare—all of the recipes in this chapter take only a few minutes to whip up.

Before we get started, note that some of the fat bombs in this chapter include raw eggs. Apart from knowing your sources well, you can make raw eggs safe for consumption by pasteurizing them: it's fast and easy, and you can learn how to do it on page 12.

Yield:
1 serving

Hands-on time:
5 mins

Overall time:
10 mins

Creamy Dark Hot Chocolate

Made with pure dark chocolate, coconut milk, and spices, this is the Holy Grail for low-carb chocolate fiends. Treat yourself to a (guilt-free!) cup the next time a craving strikes.

Ingredients

½ cup (120 ml/4 fl oz) coconut milk or heavy whipping cream

½ cup (120 ml/4 fl oz) water or almond milk

2 cardamom pods, crushed

⅛ teaspoon ground cinnamon

¼ teaspoon sugar-free vanilla extract or ⅛ teaspoon vanilla powder

Pinch salt

2 tablespoons (20 g/0.7 oz) granulated erythritol or Swerve

1 ounce (28 g) unsweetened chocolate

1 tablespoon (15 ml/0.5 fl oz) MCT oil or coconut oil

Few drops liquid stevia, to taste (optional)

Instructions

In a small saucepan, combine the coconut milk or heavy cream, water or almond milk, cardamom, cinnamon, vanilla, salt, and erythritol or Swerve. Bring to a boil. When bubbles form on top, remove the mixture from the heat and let it sit for 5 minutes. Add the unsweetened chocolate and MCT oil and let it melt while stirring. If you want a sweeter taste, add the stevia and stir again.

Pour the chocolate mixture through a sieve into a blender and pulse for a few seconds until smooth and frothy. Serve hot!

Nutrition facts per serving

Total carbs:	Fiber:	Net carbs:	Protein:	Fat:	Energy:	Calories from:
11.6 g	**4.2 g**	**7.4 g**	**6.3 g**	**52.9 g**	**528 kcal**	**Carbs (5%)** **Protein (5%)** **Fat (90%)**

Yield:
1 serving

Hands-on time:
5 mins

Overall time:
5 mins

Creamy White Hot Chocolate

Never tried white hot chocolate? Now's the time! It's just as smooth and rich as its darker counterpart, and it's full of healthy fats—and it takes just five minutes to make.

Ingredients

½ cup (120 ml/4 fl oz) coconut milk or heavy whipping cream

½ cup (120 ml/4 fl oz) water or almond milk

¼ teaspoon sugar-free vanilla extract or ⅛ teaspoon vanilla powder

Pinch salt

1 tablespoon (10 g/0.4 oz) granulated erythritol or Swerve

1 ounce (28 g) Homemade White Chocolate (page 34)

1 tablespoon (15 ml/0.5 fl oz) MCT oil or coconut oil

Few drops liquid stevia, to taste (optional)

Instructions

In a small saucepan, combine the coconut milk or heavy cream, water or almond milk, vanilla, salt, and erythritol or Swerve. Bring to a boil. When bubbles form on top, remove the mixture from the heat. Add the white chocolate and MCT oil and let it melt while stirring. If you want a sweeter taste, add the stevia and stir again. With a hand blender, pulse for a few seconds until smooth and frothy. Serve hot!

Nutrition facts per serving

Total carbs:	Fiber:	Net carbs:	Protein:	Fat:	Energy:	Calories from:
6.5 g	**0.1 g**	**6.4 g**	**3 g**	**57.8 g**	**536 kcal**	**Carbs (5%)** **Protein (2%)** **Fat (93%)**

Creamy Keto Coffee

This is an upgraded version of the popular "bulletproof" coffee, which combines butter and coconut oil for a whack of healthy fats (and an instant energy boost). Here, egg yolks—don't worry, they won't scramble—add an amazingly creamy texture and make this recipe so filling and nutritious that it can replace a regular meal.

Ingredients

1 cup (240 ml/8 fl oz) hot brewed coffee or black tea (see Tip on page 118)

1 tablespoon (15 ml/0.5 fl oz) coconut milk or heavy whipping cream

1 tablespoon (15 ml/0.5 fl oz) MCT oil or coconut oil

1 tablespoon (14 g/0.5 oz) unsalted butter or more coconut oil

¼ to ½ teaspoon ground cinnamon or vanilla powder

3 large egg yolks, whites reserved for another use

1 tablespoon (10 g/0.4 oz) granulated erythritol or Swerve, or 3 to 5 drops liquid stevia (optional)

Instructions

In a blender, combine the hot coffee or tea, coconut milk or heavy cream, MCT oil, butter, cinnamon or vanilla, and egg yolks. Pulse until smooth and frothy. If you want a sweeter taste, add the erythritol, Swerve, or stevia and pulse again. Serve hot!

Nutrition facts per serving

Total carbs:	Fiber:	Net carbs:	Protein:	Fat:	Energy:	Calories from:
2.8 g	**0.4 g**	**2.4 g**	**8.8 g**	**41.9 g**	**416 kcal**	**Carbs (2%)** **Protein (8%)** **Fat (90%)**

Yield:
1 serving

Hands-on time:
5 mins

Overall time:
5 mins

Yield:
1 serving

Hands-on time:
5 mins

Overall time:
5 mins

Fat-Burning Vanilla Smoothie

You don't need to get out the frying pan to have eggs for breakfast. It's so much faster to toss them into this thick, creamy smoothie! Combined with mascarpone cheese and a dash of coconut oil, it's a full meal in a glass.

Ingredients

2 large egg yolks, whites reserved for another use

½ cup (120 g/4.2 oz) full-fat mascarpone cheese or creamed coconut milk

¼ cup (60 ml/2 fl oz) water

4 to 5 ice cubes

1 tablespoon (15 ml/0.5 fl oz) MCT oil or coconut oil (see Tips)

1 teaspoon sugar-free vanilla extract or ½ teaspoon vanilla powder

1 tablespoon (10 g/0.4 oz) powdered erythritol or Swerve, or 3 to 5 drops liquid stevia

Whipped cream or coconut milk, for topping (optional)

Instructions

If using creamed coconut milk, make it following the instructions on page 10.

In a blender, combine the egg yolks, mascarpone or creamed coconut milk, water, ice, MCT or coconut oil, vanilla, and erythritol, Swerve, or stevia. Pulse until smooth. Top with whipped cream or coconut milk (if using).

Tips

✳ If you use coconut oil, it's important to make this using a blender to avoid leaving bits of coconut oil in your smoothie. Unlike MCT oil, coconut oil is liquid only above 75°F (24°C).

✳ If you don't eat eggs, you can still enjoy this smoothie. Use 1 tablespoon (8 g/0.3 oz) of ground chia seeds or ¼ cup (25 g/0.9 oz) whey protein powder in place of the 2 egg yolks.

Nutrition facts per serving

Total carbs:	Fiber:	Net carbs:	Protein:	Fat:	Energy:	Calories from:
4.1 g	**0 g**	**4.1 g**	**12.2 g**	**64.3 g**	**650 kcal**	**Carbs (2%)** **Protein (8%)** **Fat (90%)**

Yield:
1 serving

Hands-on time:
5 mins

Overall time:
5 mins

Raspberry and Vanilla Smoothie

This liquid fat bomb is another great breakfast option. It's loaded with raspberries, mascarpone, and good-for-you fats, and it's perfect for summer mornings when the weather's too warm for a hot meal.

Ingredients

⅓ cup (50 g/1.8 oz) raspberries, fresh or frozen

½ cup (120 g/4.2 oz) mascarpone cheese or creamed coconut milk

¼ cup (60 ml/2 fl oz) water

4 or 5 ice cubes

½ teaspoon sugar-free vanilla extract or ¼ teaspoon vanilla powder

1 tablespoon (15 ml/0.5 fl oz) MCT oil or coconut oil

1 tablespoon (10 g/0.4 oz) powdered erythritol or Swerve, or 3 to 5 drops liquid stevia (optional)

Whipped cream or coconut milk, for topping (optional)

Instructions

If using creamed coconut milk, make it following the instructions on page 10.

In a blender, combine the raspberries, mascarpone or creamed coconut milk, water, ice, vanilla, and MCT or coconut oil. Pulse until smooth. If you want a sweeter taste, add the erythritol, Swerve, or stevia, and top with whipped cream or coconut milk.

Nutrition facts per serving

Total carbs:	Fiber:	Net carbs:	Protein:	Fat:	Energy:	Calories from:
5.8 g	**1.5 g**	**4.3 g**	**7.5 g**	**55.5 g**	**552 kcal**	**Carbs (3%)** **Protein (6%)** **Fat (91%)**

Creamy Orange Smoothie

Creamy and tangy all at once, this citrusy smoothie is as refreshing as the ice pops we loved as kids—but it's far more nutritious and filling, and, of course, it's completely sugar-free.

Ingredients

2 large egg yolks, whites reserved for another use

½ cup (120 g/4.2 oz) full-fat mascarpone cheese or creamed coconut milk

¼ cup (60 ml/2 fl oz) water

4 or 5 ice cubes

1 tablespoon (15 ml/0.5 fl oz) MCT oil or coconut oil (see Tips)

1 teaspoon freshly grated orange zest or ¼ to ½ teaspoon sugar-free orange extract

¼ teaspoon ground cinnamon

1 tablespoon (10 g/0.4 oz) powdered erythritol or Swerve, or 3 to 5 drops liquid stevia

Whipped cream or coconut milk, for topping (optional)

Instructions

If using creamed coconut milk, make it following the instructions on page 10.

In a blender, combine the egg yolks, mascarpone or creamed coconut milk, water, ice, MCT or coconut oil, orange zest or extract, cinnamon, and erythritol, Swerve, or stevia. Pulse until smooth. Top with whipped cream or coconut milk (if using), and serve

Nutrition facts per serving

Total carbs:	Fiber:	Net carbs:	Protein:	Fat:	Energy:	Calories from:
4.9 g	**0.6 g**	**4.3 g**	**12.3 g**	**64.4 g**	**648 kcal**	**Carbs (3%)** **Protein (7%)** **Fat (90%)**

Yield:
1 serving

Hands-on time:
5 mins

Overall time:
5 mins

Tips

✳ If you use coconut oil, it's important to make this using a blender to avoid leaving bits of coconut oil in your smoothie. Unlike MCT oil, coconut oil is liquid only above 75°F (24°C).

✳ If you don't eat eggs, you can still enjoy this smoothie. Use 1 tablespoon (8 g/ 0.3 oz) of ground chia seeds or ¼ cup (25 g/0.9 oz) whey protein powder in place of the 2 egg yolks.

Key Lime Smoothie

Never had avocado for breakfast before? Well, there's a first time for everything! Avocados are so nutritious, plus they're a great flavor match for lime and they add a velvety texture to this satisfying low-carb smoothie.

Ingredients

½ medium (75 g/2.6 oz) ripe avocado, pitted and peeled

¼ cup (60 ml/2 fl oz) creamed coconut milk or heavy whipping cream

½ cup (120 ml/4 fl oz) water

4 or 5 ice cubes

1 tablespoon (15 ml/0.5 fl oz) MCT oil or coconut oil (see Tip)

2 tablespoons (30 ml/1 fl oz) freshly squeezed lime juice

1 teaspoon freshly grated lime zest

1 tablespoon (10 g/0.4 oz) powdered erythritol or Swerve, or 3 to 5 drops liquid stevia

Whipped cream or coconut milk, for topping (optional)

Instructions

To make creamed coconut milk, follow the instructions on page 10.

In a blender, combine the avocado, creamed coconut milk or heavy cream, water, ice, MCT or coconut oil, lime juice, lime zest, and erythritol, or Swerve, or stevia. Pulse until smooth. Top with whipped cream or coconut milk (if using), and serve.

Nutrition facts per serving

Total carbs:	Fiber:	Net carbs:	Protein:	Fat:	Energy:	Calories from:
10.1 g	**5.3 g**	**4.8 g**	**5 g**	**45.2 g**	**454 kcal**	**Carbs (4%)** **Protein (5%)** **Fat (91%)**

Yield:
1 serving

Hands-on time:
5 mins

Overall time:
5 mins

Tip
If you use coconut oil, it's important to make this using a blender to avoid leaving bits of coconut oil in your smoothie. Unlike MCT oil, coconut oil is liquid only above 75°F (24°C).

Yield:
1 serving

Hands-on time:
5 mins

Overall time:
10 mins

Almond Bliss Smoothie

Chocolate, coconut, and almond. If you're like me, they're what's in your favorite candy bar. Transform them into a healthy smoothie with this sippable fat bomb recipe.

Ingredients

½ cup (120 ml/4 fl oz) coconut milk or heavy whipping cream

½ cup (120 ml/4 fl oz) almond milk

1 tablespoon (8 g/0.3 oz) chia seeds

2 tablespoons (32 g/1.1 oz) Almond Bliss Butter (page 25)

1 tablespoon (15 ml/0.5 fl oz) MCT oil or coconut oil (see Tip)

1 tablespoon (10 g/0.4 oz) powdered erythritol or Swerve, or 3 to 5 drops liquid stevia

1 teaspoon toasted unsweetened shredded coconut or whipped cream, for topping (optional)

Instructions

In a blender, combine the coconut milk or heavy cream, almond milk, and chia seeds. Let the mixture soak for 5 to 10 minutes. Add the Almond Bliss Butter, MCT or coconut oil, and erythritol, Swerve, or stevia. Pulse until smooth and creamy. Top with toasted coconut or whipped cream (if using), and serve.

Tip

If you use coconut oil, it's important to make this using a blender to avoid leaving bits of coconut oil in your smoothie. Unlike MCT oil, coconut oil is liquid only above 75°F (24°C).

Nutrition facts per serving

Total carbs:	Fiber:	Net carbs:	Protein:	Fat:	Energy:	Calories from:
13.6 g	**6.3 g**	**7.3 g**	**8.8 g**	**53.7 g**	**548 kcal**	**Carbs (5%)** **Protein (6%)** **Fat (89%)**

Yield:
1 serving

Hands-on time:
5 mins

Overall time:
10 mins

Chocolate-Hazelnut Smoothie

You know that sugar-laden chocolate-hazelnut spread that's so good when it's slathered on—well, just about anything? Add my homemade version to a smoothie: it's even better than the store-bought stuff, and it means and you get chocolate for breakfast. Don't worry; it's low-carb and sugar-free!

Ingredients

½ cup (120 ml/4 fl oz) coconut milk or heavy whipping cream

¼ cup (60 ml/2 fl oz) water

1 tablespoon (8 g/0.3 oz) chia seeds

2 tablespoons (32 g/1.1 oz) Chocolate-Hazelnut Butter (page 20)

1 tablespoon (15 ml/0.5 fl oz) MCT oil or coconut oil (see Tip on page 148)

1 tablespoon (10 g/0.4 oz) powdered erythritol or Swerve, or 3 to 5 drops liquid stevia

4 or 5 ice cubes (optional)

Instructions

In a blender, combine the coconut milk or heavy cream, water, and chia seeds. Let the mixture soak for 5 to 10 minutes. Add the Chocolate-Hazelnut Butter, MCT or coconut oil, and erythritol, Swerve, or stevia. Pulse until smooth and creamy. Serve over ice, if you like.

Nutrition facts per serving

Total carbs:	Fiber:	Net carbs:	Protein:	Fat:	Energy:	Calories from:
12.8 g	**5.7 g**	**7.1 g**	**7.8 g**	**58.4 g**	**570 kcal**	**Carbs (5%)** **Protein (5%)** **Fat (90%)**

Lemon Cheesecake Smoothie

Who said breakfast shouldn't taste like dessert? Not me! Satisfy your sweet tooth first thing in the morning with this scrumptious-but-sating smoothie.

Ingredients

¼ cup (60 g/2.1 oz) full-fat cream cheese or creamed coconut milk

¼ cup (60 ml/2 fl oz) heavy whipping cream or coconut milk

½ cup (120 ml/4 fl oz) water

2 tablespoons (30 ml/1 fl oz) freshly squeezed lemon juice

1 teaspoon freshly grated lemon zest

1 tablespoon (15 ml/0.5 fl oz) MCT oil or coconut oil (see Tip)

1 tablespoon (10 g/0.4 oz) powdered erythritol or Swerve, or 3 to 5 drops liquid stevia

4 or 5 ice cubes (optional)

Instructions

If using creamed coconut milk, make it following the instructions on page 10.

In a blender, combine the cream cheese or creamed coconut milk, cream or coconut milk, water, lemon juice, lemon zest, MCT or coconut oil, and erythritol, Swerve, or stevia. Pulse until smooth and creamy. Serve over ice, if you like.

Tip

If you use coconut oil, it's important to make this using a blender to avoid leaving bits of coconut oil in your smoothie. Unlike MCT oil, coconut oil is liquid only above 75°F (24°C).

Nutrition facts per serving

Total carbs:	Fiber:	Net carbs:	Protein:	Fat:	Energy:	Calories from:
6.1 g	**0.4 g**	**5.7 g**	**5.5 g**	**52.7 g**	**490 kcal**	**Carbs (4%)** **Protein (4%)** **Fat (92%)**

Pumpkin Pie Smoothie

Pumpkin only gets top billing in supermarket shelves in the fall—which isn't quite fair, since it's delicious year-round. It's also a great addition to just about anything, including this keto-friendly smoothie. Featured here are my homemade Pumpkin and Sun Butter, sugar-free pumpkin purée, and aromatic autumnal spices.

Ingredients

¼ cup (60 g/2.1 oz) full-fat cream cheese or creamed coconut milk

¼ cup (60 ml/2 fl oz) heavy whipping cream or coconut milk

½ cup (120 ml/4 fl oz) water

1 tablespoon (16 g/0.5 oz) Pumpkin Sun Butter (page 31)

2 tablespoons (40 g/1.4 oz) unsweetened pumpkin purée

½ teaspoon pumpkin pie spice mix

1 tablespoon (15 ml/0.5 fl oz) MCT oil or coconut oil (see Tip)

1 tablespoon (10 g/0.4 oz) powdered erythritol or Swerve, or 3 to 5 drops liquid stevia

4 or 5 ice cubes (optional)

Instructions

If using creamed coconut milk, make it following the instructions on page 10.

In a blender, combine the cream cheese or creamed coconut milk, cream or coconut milk, water, Pumpkin Sun Butter, pumpkin purée, pumpkin pie spice mix, MCT or coconut oil, and erythritol, Swerve, or stevia. Pulse until smooth and creamy. Serve over ice, if you like.

Nutrition facts per serving

Total carbs:	Fiber:	Net carbs:	Protein:	Fat:	Energy:	Calories from:
11.2 g	**3.3 g**	**7.9 g**	**9.5 g**	**60.7 g**	**587 kcal**	**Carbs (5%)** **Protein (6%)** **Fat (89%)**

Yield:
1 serving

Hands-on time:
5 mins

Overall time:
5 mins

Tip
If you use coconut oil, it's important to make this using a blender to avoid leaving bits of coconut oil in your smoothie. Unlike MCT oil, coconut oil is liquid only above 75°F (24°C).

Chapter 6

Savory Fat Bombs

No sweet tooth? No problem! In this chapter, you'll learn to make delicious, savory fat bombs that take their inspiration from everything from pepperoni pizza to cheesy jalapeño poppers to smoked salmon pâté. Most of these recipes do contain cheese or butter, but I've included some dairy-free recipes, too. You can eat these fat bombs on their own, but they're also great served atop fresh cucumber slices, lettuce leaves, or crispy bacon slices. And most can even be used as spreads for low-carb bread! (If you're looking for recipes for homemade, grain-free paleo bread, check out my book *The KetoDiet Cookbook* (Fair Winds Press), or visit my blog at www.ketodietapp.com/blog.

Easy Savory Fat Bombs

Garlic and spring onion add plenty of flavor to these simple savory fat bombs. For extra crunch, serve them on top of lettuce leaves or crispy bacon slices.

Ingredients

3.5 ounces (100 g) full-fat cream cheese, at room temperature

¼ cup (56 g/2 oz) unsalted butter, at room temperature

2 bacon slices (60 g/2.1 oz)

1 garlic clove, crushed

1 medium (15 g/0.5 oz) spring onion, sliced

Pinch salt

Pinch pepper

Crispy lettuce leaves, for serving (optional)

Instructions

In a bowl, mash together the cream cheese and butter, or process in a food processor until smooth.

Preheat the oven to 325°F (160°C, or gas mark 3). Line a rimmed baking sheet with parchment paper. Be sure to use a rimmed sheet to contain the bacon fat, as you'll need it for the recipe, too. Lay the bacon strips flat on the parchment, leaving enough space between so they don't overlap.

Place the sheet in the preheated oven and cook for 25 to 30 minutes, or until the bacon is golden brown. Remove from the oven and cool slightly before crumbling into the pan. Set aside a small amount of crumbled bacon for topping.

To the cream cheese and butter mixture, add the garlic, sliced onion, bacon, and bacon grease from the sheet. Season with salt and pepper. Mix well to combine.

Nutrition facts per serving (1 fat bomb)

Total carbs:	Fiber:	Net carbs:	Protein:	Fat:	Energy:	Calories from:
0.9 g	**0.1 g**	**0.8 g**	**2.7 g**	**14.6 g**	**136 kcal**	**Carbs (2%)** **Protein (7%)** **Fat (91%)**

Yield:
6 fat bombs

Hands-on time:
10 mins

Overall time:
30 mins + chilling time

Line a clean sheet with parchment. Create 6 small mounds of the mixture, about 2 tablespoons (40 g/1.4 oz) each, place them on the prepared sheet, and top with the reserved bacon. Refrigerate for 30 minutes to 1 hour, or until set. Alternatively, simply transfer the mixture to an airtight container and refrigerate. When ready to serve, just spoon out 2 tablespoons (40 g/1.4 oz) per serving and serve on top of lettuce leaves (if using). Keep refrigerated for up to 5 days.

Pepperoni Pizza Fat Bombs

These keto-friendly fat bombs are every bit as good as delivery pepperoni pizza—minus the carb-laden crust, of course!

Ingredients

3.5 ounces (100 g) full-fat cream cheese, at room temperature

¼ cup (56 g/2 oz) unsalted butter, at room temperature

12 (36 g/1.3 oz) pepperoni slices

1 garlic clove, minced

½ small red pepper (40 g/ 1.4 oz), finely chopped

¼ cup (28 g/1 oz) grated mozzarella cheese

1 to 2 tablespoons (5 to 10 g/ 0.2 to 0.4 oz) chopped fresh herbs (such as basil, oregano, thyme), or 1 to 2 teaspoons dried herbs

⅛ teaspoon chili powder

Pinch salt

⅓ cup (30 g/1.1 oz) grated Parmesan cheese

Instructions

In a bowl, mash together the cream cheese and the butter with a fork, or process in a food processor until smooth.

In a large skillet set over medium heat, cook the pepperoni slices on both sides until crispy. Transfer to a plate to cool.

Add the garlic and red pepper to the pepperoni juices in the skillet and cook for a few minutes over medium heat until fragrant. Remove from the heat and cool slightly. Add to the cream cheese and butter mixture and mix well with an electric beater or a hand whisk.

Add the grated mozzarella cheese, herbs, chili powder, and salt. Mix well again. Refrigerate for 20 to 30 minutes, or until set.

Using a large spoon or an ice cream scoop, divide the mixture into 6 balls. Roll each ball in the Parmesan cheese and place on top of 2 slices of crisped pepperoni. Enjoy immediately or refrigerate in an airtight container for up to 5 days.

Nutrition facts per serving (1 fat bomb)

Total carbs:	Fiber:	Net carbs:	Protein:	Fat:	Energy:	Calories from:
1.5 g	**0.2 g**	**1.3 g**	**5.7 g**	**17.2 g**	**175 kcal**	**Carbs (3%)** **Protein (12%)** **Fat (85%)**

Yield:
6 fat bombs

Hands-on time:
15 mins

Overall time:
**20 mins +
chilling time**

Sweet and Savory Fat Bombs

Yield:
6 fat bombs

Hands-on time:
15 mins

Overall time:
15 mins + chilling time

Stilton and Chive Fat Bombs

Blue cheese addicts will adore these zero-carb fat bombs, in which pungent Stilton is suspended in a cloud of cream cheese and butter. The final flourish comes from a thorough coating of freshly chopped chives.

Ingredients

3.5 ounces (100 g) full-fat cream cheese, at room temperature

¼ cup (56 g/2 oz) unsalted butter, at room temperature

½ cup (65 g/2.3 oz) crumbled Stilton or other blue cheese

2 medium (30 g/1.1 oz) spring onions, finely chopped

1 tablespoon (3 g/0.1 oz) finely chopped fresh parsley

⅓ cup (30 g/1.1 oz) chopped fresh chives, or more finely chopped spring onion

Instructions

In a bowl, mash together the cream cheese and butter, or process in a food processor until smooth.

Add the crumbled blue cheese, spring onions, and parsley. Mix until well combined. Refrigerate for 20 to 30 minutes, or until set.

Using a large spoon or an ice cream scoop, divide the mixture into 6 balls. Roll each ball in the chopped chives and place on a plate. Enjoy immediately or refrigerate in an airtight container for up to 5 days.

Nutrition facts per serving (1 fat bomb)

Total carbs:	Fiber:	Net carbs:	Protein:	Fat:	Energy:	Calories from:
1.1 g	**0.2 g**	**0.8 g**	**5 g**	**16.2 g**	**157 kcal**	**Carbs (2%)** **Protein (11%)** **Fat (87%)**

Yield:
6 fat bombs

Hands-on time:
15 mins

Overall time:
**15 mins +
chilling time**

Tomato and Olive Fat Bombs

**Every bit as delicious as *pasta puttanesca*, these fat bombs are packed with
Mediterranean flavors and encrusted with crunchy flaked almonds.**

Ingredients

3.5 ounces (100 g) full-fat
cream cheese, at room
temperature

¼ cup (56 g/2 oz) unsalted
butter, at room temperature

¼ cup (30 g/1.1 oz) grated
Manchego cheese

¼ cup (28 g/1 oz) drained,
chopped sun-dried tomatoes

¼ cup (25 g/0.9 oz) pitted,
sliced olives

2 tablespoons (18 g/0.6 oz)
capers, drained

1 garlic clove, crushed

Pepper, to taste

⅓ cup (30 g/1.1 oz) flaked
almonds, raw or toasted

Instructions

In a bowl, mash together the cream cheese and
butter, or process in a food processor until smooth.

Add the Manchego cheese, sun-dried tomatoes,
olives, capers, and garlic. Mix until well combined.
Season with pepper. Refrigerate for 20 to 30 minutes,
or until set.

Using a large spoon or an ice cream scoop, divide
the mixture into 6 balls. Roll each ball in the almond
flakes. Enjoy immediately or refrigerate in an airtight
container for up to 5 days.

Nutrition facts per serving (1 fat bomb)

Total carbs:	Fiber:	Net carbs:	Protein:	Fat:	Energy:	Calories from:
3 g	**1.1 g**	**1.9 g**	**4.2 g**	**18.1 g**	**178 kcal**	**Carbs (4%)** **Protein (9%)** **Fat (87%)**

Ham and Cheese Fat Bombs

There are few things that can't be improved by a cloak of sweet-and-salty Parma ham—and these creamy, basil-flecked fat bombs are no exception. Try them as a low-carb afternoon snack.

Ingredients

3.5 ounces (100 g) full-fat cream cheese, at room temperature

¼ cup (56 g/2 oz) unsalted butter, at room temperature

¼ cup (30 g/1.1 oz) grated Cheddar cheese or Gouda cheese

2 tablespoons (10 g/0.4 oz) chopped fresh basil

Pepper, to taste

6 slices (90 g/3.2 oz) Parma ham

6 large (30 g/1.1 oz) green olives, pitted

Instructions

In a bowl, mash together the cream cheese and butter, or process in a food processor until smooth.

Add the Cheddar cheese and basil. Mix until well combined. Season with pepper. Refrigerate for 20 to 30 minutes, or until set.

Using a large spoon or an ice-cream scoop, divide the mixture into 6 balls. Wrap each ball in 1 slice of Parma ham and place on a plate. Top each ball with 1 olive and pierce with a toothpick to hold it in place. Enjoy immediately or refrigerate in an airtight container for up to 5 days.

Nutrition facts per serving (1 fat bomb)

Total carbs:	Fiber:	Net carbs:	Protein:	Fat:	Energy:	Calories from:
0.9 g	**0.2 g**	**0.7 g**	**6.4 g**	**16.4 g**	**167 kcal**	**Carbs (2%)** **Protein (14%)** **Fat (84%)**

Veggie and Cheese Fat Bombs

Just like a gourmet vegetable pizza only sans carbs, these tasty fat bombs feature caramelized onion, porcini mushrooms, fresh spinach, and goat cheese.

Ingredients

3.5 ounces (100 g) full-fat cream cheese, at room temperature

¼ cup (56 g/2 oz) unsalted butter, at room temperature

1 tablespoon (15 g/0.5 oz) ghee

½ small white onion (35 g/1.2 oz), peeled and finely chopped

1 garlic clove, peeled and finely chopped

½ cup (15 g/0.5 oz) dried porcini mushrooms, soaked in 1 cup (240 ml/8.1 fl oz) warm water for 30 minutes, then drained and sliced

2 cups (60 g/2.1 oz) fresh spinach

Salt, to taste

Pepper to taste

¼ cup (30 g/2.1 oz) grated hard goat cheese

Instructions

In a bowl, mash together the cream cheese and butter, or process in a food processor until smooth.

Grease a hot pan with the ghee. Add the onion and garlic and cook over medium heat for 2 to 3 minutes, or until fragrant. Add the mushrooms and cook for about 2 minutes more. Add the spinach and cook for 1 minute more, or until wilted. Remove the pan from the heat and set aside to cool.

To the cream cheese and butter, add the cooled mushroom and spinach mixture. Mix until well combined. Season with salt and pepper. Refrigerate for 20 to 30 minutes, or until set.

Using a large spoon or an ice cream scoop, divide the mixture into 6 balls. Roll each ball in the goat cheese. Enjoy immediately or refrigerate in an airtight container for up to 5 days.

Nutrition facts per serving (1 fat bomb)

Total carbs:	Fiber:	Net carbs:	Protein:	Fat:	Energy:	Calories from:
3.6 g	**0.6 g**	**3 g**	**3.4 g**	**16.7 g**	**166 kcal**	**Carbs (7%)** **Protein (8%)** **Fat (85%)**

Yield:
6 fat bombs

Hands-on time:
15 mins

Overall time:
**45 mins +
chilling time**

Herbed Cheese Fat Bombs

Reach for one of these cheesy fat bombs next time you're craving a snack. They're infused with garlic and fresh herbs and coated in Parmesan cheese, and they're incredibly satisfying.

Ingredients

3.5 ounces (100 g) full-fat cream cheese, at room temperature

¼ cup (56 g/2 oz) unsalted butter, at room temperature

4 pieces (12 g/0.4 oz) sun-dried tomatoes, drained and chopped

4 (12 g/0.4 oz) pitted olives such as kalamatas, chopped

2 to 3 tablespoons (10 g/0.4 oz) chopped fresh herbs (such as basil, thyme, and oregano), or 2 teaspoons dried herbs

2 garlic cloves, crushed

Salt, to taste

Pepper, to taste

5 tablespoons (25 g/0.9 oz) grated Parmesan cheese

Instructions

In a bowl, mash together the cream cheese and butter, or process in a food processor until smooth.

Add the sun-dried tomatoes, olives, herbs, and garlic. Season with salt and pepper. Mix well to combine. Refrigerate for 20 to 30 minutes, or until set.

Using a large spoon or an ice cream scoop, divide the mixture into 5 balls. Roll each ball in the Parmesan cheese. Enjoy immediately or refrigerate in an airtight container for up to 1 week.

Nutrition facts per serving (1 fat bomb)

Total carbs:	Fiber:	Net carbs:	Protein:	Fat:	Energy:	Calories from:
2 g	**0.3 g**	**1.7 g**	**3.7 g**	**17.1 g**	**164 kcal**	**Carbs (4%)** **Protein (8%)** **Fat (88%)**

Yield:
5 fat bombs

Hands-on time:
10 mins

Overall time:
**10 mins +
chilling time**

Sweet and Savory Fat Bombs

Yield:	Hands-on time:	Overall time:
6 fat bombs	**15 mins**	**15 mins + chilling time**

Waldorf Salad Fat Bombs

There's only one thing to do when you've got pecans, cheese, and green apples lurking in your kitchen. Make these sugar-free, bite-size fat bombs!

Ingredients

3 ounces (85 g) full-fat cream cheese, at room temperature

2 tablespoons (28 g/1 oz) unsalted butter or ghee, at room temperature

½ cup (65 g/2.3 oz) crumbled blue cheese

½ small (60 g/2.1 oz) green apple, diced into ½-inch pieces

¼ teaspoon garlic powder

¼ teaspoon onion powder

2 tablespoons (5 g/0.2 oz) chopped fresh chives or spring onion

Salt, to taste

Pepper, to taste

⅔ cup (70 g/2.5 oz) pecans or walnuts, roughly chopped

Instructions

In a bowl, mash together the cream cheese and butter or ghee, or process in a food processor until smooth.

Add the crumbled blue cheese, apple, garlic powder, onion powder, and chives. Stir to combine. Season with salt and pepper. Refrigerate for 20 to 30 minutes, or until set.

Using a large spoon or an ice cream scoop, divide the mixture into 6 balls. Roll each ball in the pecans. Enjoy immediately or refrigerate in an airtight container for up to 1 week.

Nutrition facts per serving (1 fat bomb)

Total carbs:	Fiber:	Net carbs:	Protein:	Fat:	Energy:	Calories from:
4 g	**1.4 g**	**2.5 g**	**4.5 g**	**19.3 g**	**193 kcal**	**Carbs (5%)** **Protein (9%)** **Fat (86%)**

Brie Cheese Fat Bombs

Rich, buttery brie is the star of the show in these easy-to-make fat bombs. Serve as a dip with raw vegetables or try them on their own atop crisp lettuce leaves.

Ingredients

2 ounces (56 g) full-fat cream cheese, at room temperature

¼ cup (56 g/2 oz) unsalted butter or ghee, at room temperature

½ cup (70 g/2.5 oz) chopped brie cheese or Camembert cheese

1 tablespoon (15 g/0.5 oz) ghee

1 small (70 g/2.5 oz) white onion, diced

1 garlic clove, minced

½ teaspoon paprika

Salt, to taste

Pepper, to taste

Crispy lettuce leaves, for serving (optional)

Instructions

In a bowl, mash together the cream cheese and butter or ghee, or process in a food processor until smooth. Add the cheese and stir to combine.

Grease a hot pan with the ghee. Add onion and garlic and cook for 2 to 3 minutes over medium heat, or until fragrant. Remove from the heat and cool. Once cooled, add to the cheese and butter mixture.

Stir in the paprika and season with salt and pepper. Refrigerate for 20 to 30 minutes, or until set.

Using a large spoon or an ice cream scoop, divide the mixture into 6 mounds and serve on top of lettuce leaves (if using). Enjoy immediately, or refrigerate without lettuce leaves in an airtight container for up to 1 week.

Nutrition facts per serving (1 fat bomb)

Total carbs:	Fiber:	Net carbs:	Protein:	Fat:	Energy:	Calories from:
1.7 g	**0.3 g**	**1.4 g**	**3.3 g**	**16.1 g**	**158 kcal**	**Carbs (4%)** **Protein (8%)** **Fat (88%)**

Yield:
6 fat bombs

Hands-on time:
10 mins

Overall time:
**10 mins +
chilling time**

Pork Belly Fat Bombs

If you're lucky enough to have leftover pork belly, use it to make these snack-size fat bombs. They're meaty and filling and, since they're laced with mustard and horseradish, they also pack quite a kick!

Ingredients

6 pancetta slices or 3 bacon slices (90 g/3.2 oz), cut in half widthwise

5.3 ounces (150 g) cooked pork belly (see Tip)

¼ cup (55 g/1.9 oz) mayonnaise, preferably homemade

1 tablespoon (15 g/0.5 oz) Dijon mustard

1 tablespoon (15 g/0.5 oz) grated fresh horseradish

Salt, to taste

Pepper, to taste

Crispy lettuce leaves, for serving (optional)

Instructions

Preheat the oven to 325°F (160°C, or gas mark 3). Line a baking sheet with parchment paper. Lay the pancetta or bacon slices flat on the parchment, leaving enough space between so they don't overlap. Place the sheet in the preheated oven and cook for 25 to 30 minutes, or until crispy. The exact amount of cooking time depends on the thickness of the pancetta or bacon slices. Remove from the oven and set aside to cool. Pour the bacon grease into a glass container and reserve for another use, such as frying eggs. When cool enough to handle, crumble the pancetta or bacon into a dish and set aside.

Shred the pork belly into a bowl. Mix in the mayonnaise, mustard, and horseradish. Season with salt and pepper. Divide the mixture into 6 mounds. Top with the crumbled pancetta or bacon and serve on top of crispy lettuce leaves (if using). Enjoy immediately or refrigerate in an airtight container for up to 5 days.

Nutrition facts per serving (1 fat bomb)

Total carbs:	Fiber:	Net carbs:	Protein:	Fat:	Energy:	Calories from:
0.5 g	0.2 g	0.3 g	5.8 g	26.4 g	263 kcal	Carbs (1%) Protein (9%) Fat (90%)

Yield:
6 fat bombs

Hands-on time:
10 mins

Overall time:
**2 hours
30 mins**

Tip

If you need to cook the pork belly, preheat the oven to 400°F (200°C, or gas mark 6). Using a sharp knife, score the pork skin down to the meat in several places. Make the cuts close together and try not to cut the meat. Place it in a deep roasting pan and into the preheated oven. Cook for 30 minutes. Reduce the temperature to 325°F (160°C, or gas mark 3), and cook for 1 hour, 30 minutes more. Finally, increase the temperature to 425°F (220°C, or gas mark 7), and cook for another 30 minutes. Remove from the oven and set aside to cool at room temperature.

Yield:
6 fat bombs

Hands-on time:
10 mins

Overall time:
30 mins + chilling time

Cheesy Jalapeño Fat Bombs

These fat bombs were inspired by jalapeño poppers, those lethally addictive bar snacks. Be forewarned, my healthy, low-carb version is even better. For extra texture and flavor, I use crispy bacon bits instead of breading or batter coating—no deep-frying necessary!

Ingredients

3.5 ounces (100 g) full-fat cream cheese, at room temperature

¼ cup (55 g/2 oz) unsalted butter or ghee, at room temperature

4 bacon slices (120 g/4.2 oz)

¼ cup (30 g/1.1 oz) grated Gruyère cheese or Cheddar cheese

2 (28 g/1 oz) jalapeño peppers, halved, seeded, and finely chopped

Instructions

In a bowl, mash together the cream cheese and butter or ghee, or process in a food processor until smooth.

Preheat the oven to 325°F (160°C, or gas mark 3). Line a rimmed baking sheet with parchment paper. Be sure to use a rimmed sheet to contain the bacon fat, as you'll need it for the recipe, too. Lay the bacon slices flat on the parchment, leaving enough space between so they don't overlap. Place the sheet in the preheated oven and cook for 25 to 30 minutes, or until crispy. The exact amount of cooking time depends on the thickness of the bacon slices. Remove from the oven and set aside to cool. When cool enough to handle, crumble the bacon into a bowl and set aside.

To the cream cheese and butter mixture, add the Gruyère or Cheddar cheese, jalapeños, and bacon grease. Mix well to combine. Refrigerate for 30 minutes to 1 hour, or until set.

Divide the mixture into 6 fat bombs and place them on a parchment-lined plate. If serving immediately, roll them in the crumbled bacon until well coated. If serving later, refrigerate without the bacon coating in an airtight container for up to 1 week. Roll the fat bombs in freshly cooked or reheated bacon crumbs just before serving.

Nutrition facts per serving (1 fat bomb)

Total carbs:	Fiber:	Net carbs:	Protein:	Fat:	Energy:	Calories from:
0.9 g	**0.2 g**	**0.7 g**	**3.5 g**	**15 g**	**142 kcal**	**Carbs (4%)** **Protein (4%)** **Fat (92%)**

Yield:
6 fat bombs

Hands-on time:
10 mins

Overall time:
30 mins + chilling time

Bacon and Egg Fat Bombs

Bacon and eggs aren't just for breakfast anymore—when you've got a batch of these filling fat bombs stashed in the fridge, you can enjoy them any time of day!

Ingredients

4 large bacon slices (120 g/ 4.2 oz)

2 large hardboiled eggs, cooled, peeled, and quartered

¼ cup (56 g/2 oz) unsalted butter or ghee, at room temperature

2 tablespoons (30 g/1.1 oz) mayonnaise, preferably homemade

Salt, to taste

Pepper, to taste

Instructions

Preheat the oven to 325°F (160°C, or gas mark 3). Line a rimmed baking sheet with parchment paper. Be sure to use a rimmed sheet to contain the bacon fat, as you'll need it for the recipe, too. Lay the bacon slices flat on the parchment, leaving enough space between so they don't overlap. Place the sheet in the preheated oven and cook for 25 to 30 minutes, or until crispy. The exact amount of cooking time depends on the thickness of the bacon slices. Remove from the oven and set aside to cool. When cool enough to handle, crumble the bacon into a bowl and set aside.

In another bowl, mash the eggs and butter or ghee together.

Stir in the mayonnaise. Season with salt and pepper and mix well. Pour in the bacon grease and mix again. Refrigerate for 20 to 30 minutes, or until set.

Using a large spoon or an ice cream scoop, divide the mixture into 6 balls. If serving immediately, roll them in the crumbled bacon. If serving later, refrigerate without the bacon coating in an airtight container for up to 5 days. Roll the fat bombs in freshly cooked or reheated bacon crumbs just before serving.

Nutrition facts per serving (1 fat bomb)

Total carbs:	Fiber:	Net carbs:	Protein:	Fat:	Energy:	Calories from:
0.2 g	**0 g**	**0.2 g**	**5 g**	**18.4 g**	**185 kcal**	**Carbs (0%)** **Protein (11%)** **Fat (89%)**

Yield:	Hands-on time:	Overall time:
6 fat bombs	**10 mins**	**30 mins + chilling time**

Bacon and Guacamole Fat Bombs

There's only one way to improve upon homemade guacamole, and that's to transform it into bacon-coated fat bombs. Seriously.

Ingredients

4 large bacon slices (120 g/ 4.2 oz)

½ large (100 g/3.5 oz) avocado, halved, pitted, and peeled

¼ cup (56 g/2 oz) unsalted butter or ghee, at room temperature

2 garlic cloves, crushed

1 small chile pepper, finely chopped

1 tablespoon (15 ml/0.5 fl oz) fresh lime juice

Salt, to taste

Pepper, to taste

½ small (35 g/1.2 oz) white onion, diced

Instructions

Preheat the oven to 325°F (160°C, or gas mark 3). Line a rimmed baking sheet with parchment paper. Be sure to use a rimmed sheet to contain the bacon fat, as you'll need it for the recipe, too. Lay the bacon strips flat on the parchment, leaving enough space between so they don't overlap. Place the sheet in the preheated oven and cook for 25 to 30 minutes, or until crispy. The exact amount of cooking time depends on the thickness of the bacon slices. Remove from the oven and set aside to cool. When cool enough to handle, crumble the bacon into a bowl and set aside.

In a bowl, combine the avocado, butter or ghee, garlic, chile pepper, and lime juice. Season with salt and pepper. Mash with a potato masher or fork until well combined. Stir in the onion. Pour in the bacon grease from the baking sheet and mix well. Cover with aluminum foil and refrigerate for 20 to 30 minutes.

Using a large spoon or an ice cream scoop, divide the mixture into 6 balls. If serving immediately, roll them in the crumbled bacon. If serving later, refrigerate without the bacon coating in an airtight container for up to 5 days. Roll the fat bombs in freshly cooked or reheated bacon crumbs just before serving.

Nutrition facts per serving (1 fat bomb)

Total carbs:	Fiber:	Net carbs:	Protein:	Fat:	Energy:	Calories from:
2.7 g	**1.3 g**	**1.4 g**	**3.4 g**	**15.2 g**	**156 kcal**	**Carbs (3%)** **Protein (9%)** **Fat (88%)**

Bacon and Pâté Fat Bombs

Not a fan of liver? Well, these fat bombs are likely to change your mind—not least because they're covered in bacon bits, which make just about everything irresistible.

Ingredients

4 large bacon slices (120 g/ 4.2 oz)

⅓ cup (75 g/2.6 oz) ghee or unsalted butter, at room temperature, divided

5.3 ounces (150 g) chicken livers, diced

½ medium (56 g/2 oz) white onion, diced

2 garlic cloves, finely chopped

1 tablespoon (5 g/0.2 oz) chopped fresh sage

Pinch mace

Salt, to taste

Pepper, to taste

Instructions

Preheat the oven to 325°F (160°C, or gas mark 3). Line a rimmed baking sheet with parchment paper. Be sure to use a rimmed sheet to contain the bacon fat, as you'll need it for the recipe, too. Lay the bacon strips flat on the parchment, leaving enough space between so they don't overlap. Place the sheet in the preheated oven and cook for 25 to 30 minutes, or until crispy. The exact amount of cooking time depends on the thickness of the bacon slices. Remove from the oven and set aside to cool. When cool enough to handle, crumble the bacon into a bowl and set aside.

In a skillet, heat half of the ghee or butter. Add the livers. Cook for 3 to 5 minutes over high heat, or until they're crisp on the outside but still slightly pink in the middle. Transfer to a blender and pulse until smooth.

In a clean skillet, combine the remaining ghee or butter, onion, and garlic. Cook for about 10 minutes over medium heat,

Nutrition facts per serving (1 fat bomb)

Total carbs:	Fiber:	Net carbs:	Protein:	Fat:	Energy:	Calories from:
1.4 g	**0.2 g**	**1.2 g**	**7 g**	**19.8 g**	**213 kcal**	**Carbs (2%)** **Protein (13%)** **Fat (85%)**

Yield:
6 fat bombs

Hands-on time:
10 mins

Overall time:
30 mins + chilling time

stirring frequently. Transfer to the blender with the puréed chicken livers. Add the sage, mace, and the bacon grease from the baking sheet, and pulse until smooth. Season with salt and pepper. Cover with aluminum foil and refrigerate for 20 to 30 minutes.

Using a large spoon or an ice cream scoop, divide the mixture into 6 balls. If serving immediately, roll them in the crumbled bacon. If serving later, refrigerate without the bacon coating in an airtight container for up to 5 days. Roll the fat bombs in freshly cooked or reheated bacon crumbs just before serving.

Yield:
6 fat bombs

Hands-on time:
10 mins

Overall time:
10 mins + chilling time

Salmon Pâté Fat Bombs

Smoked salmon and cream cheese—partners in crime—are at their best when dressed up with lemon and dill. This simple recipe shows you how to transform that classic combination into fabulous keto-friendly fat bombs.

Ingredients

3.5 ounces (100 g) full-fat cream cheese, at room temperature

⅓ cup (75 g/2.7 oz) unsalted butter or ghee, at room temperature

1 small package (50 g/1.8 oz) smoked salmon

1 tablespoon (15 ml/0.5 fl oz) fresh lemon juice

2 tablespoons (8 g/0.3 oz) chopped fresh dill, plus additional for garnishing

Pepper, to taste

Crispy lettuce leaves, for serving (optional)

Instructions

In a food processor, combine the cream cheese, butter or ghee, smoked salmon, lemon juice, dill, and pepper. Pulse until smooth.

Line a baking sheet with parchment paper. Spoon about 2 tablespoons (40 g/1.4 oz) of the mixture per portion onto the prepared sheet. Garnish each with more dill. Refrigerate for 20 to 30 minutes, or until set. Alternatively, transfer the mixture to an airtight container and refrigerate. When ready to serve, spoon out 2 tablespoons (40 g/1.4 oz) per serving and serve on top of lettuce leaves (if using). Keep refrigerated in an airtight container for up to 1 week.

Nutrition facts per serving (1 fat bomb)

Total carbs:	Fiber:	Net carbs:	Protein:	Fat:	Energy:	Calories from:
0.8 g	**0.1 g**	**0.7 g**	**3.2 g**	**15.7 g**	**147 kcal**	**Carbs (2%)** **Protein (8%)** **Fat (90%)**

Yield:	Hands-on time:	Overall time:
6 fat bombs	**10 mins**	**10 mins + chilling time**

Anchovy Fat Bombs

Okay, so anchovy isn't for everyone, but I love it—and the fact that it's packed with healthy fats is a big plus, too. Try it in this easy-to-prepare tapenade, where its assertiveness is balanced by other strong flavors, like garlic, parsley, and cheese.

Ingredients

3.5 ounces (100 g) full-fat cream cheese, at room temperature

¼ cup (56 g/2 oz) unsalted butter, at room temperature

1 ounce (28 g) canned anchovies, drained

1 garlic clove, crushed

1 tablespoon (3 g/0.1 oz) chopped fresh parsley

¼ cup (28 g/1 oz) shredded Cheddar cheese

⅓ cup (30 g/1.1 oz) flaked almonds

Cucumber slices, for serving (optional)

Instructions

In a food processor, combine the cream cheese, butter, anchovies, garlic, and parsley. Pulse until smooth. Transfer to a bowl and add the Cheddar cheese and almonds and mix with a spoon.

Refrigerate for 20 to 30 minutes, or until set. Enjoy as a dip with sliced cucumber, or keep refrigerated in an airtight container for up to 1 week.

Nutrition facts per serving (1 fat bomb)

Total carbs:	Fiber:	Net carbs:	Protein:	Fat:	Energy:	Calories from:
1.8 g	**0.7 g**	**1.1 g**	**5.1 g**	**17.2 g**	**170 kcal**	**Carbs (3%)** **Protein (11%)** **Fat (86%)**

Yield:
6 fat bombs

Hands-on time:
10 mins

Overall time:
10 mins + chilling time

Smoked Mackerel Pâté Fat Bombs

If you're a fan of smoked fish, you're sure to love this low-carb dip. It's lightened and brightened by a dash of fresh lime juice and a handful of chives.

Ingredients

3.5 ounces (100 g) full-fat cream cheese, at room temperature

¼ cup (56 g/2 oz) unsalted butter, at room temperature

1 medium (100 g/3.5 oz) smoked mackerel fillet

1 tablespoon (15 ml/0.5 fl oz) freshly squeezed lime juice

2 tablespoons (8 g/0.3 oz) chopped fresh chives

Cucumber slices, for serving (optional)

Instructions

In a food processor, combine the cream cheese, butter, mackerel, and lime juice. Pulse until smooth. Transfer to a bowl, add the chives, and mix with a spoon. Refrigerate for 20 to 30 minutes, or until set. Enjoy as a dip with cucumber slices, or refrigerate in an airtight container for up to 1 week.

Nutrition facts per serving (1 fat bomb)

Total carbs:	Fiber:	Net carbs:	Protein:	Fat:	Energy:	Calories from:
0.8 g	**0.1 g**	**0.7 g**	**4.9 g**	**16.5 g**	**161 kcal**	**Carbs (2%)** **Protein (11%)** **Fat (87%)**

Yield:
5 fat bombs

Hands-on time:
10 mins

Overall time:
10 mins

Sardine Fat Bombs

Two superfoods in a single fat bomb? That's right! Sardines are rich in vitamins, minerals, and omega-3s, while certain compounds found in turmeric may act as powerful antioxidants.

Ingredients

3.5 ounces (100 g) sardines, drained

2 tablespoons (28 g/1 oz) unsalted butter or ghee, at room temperature

2 tablespoons (30 g/1.1 oz) mayonnaise, preferably homemade

½ teaspoon powdered turmeric

½ small (30 g/1.1 oz) white onion, diced

1 tablespoon (15 ml/0.5 fl oz) freshly squeezed lemon juice

2 tablespoons (30 m/1 fl oz) extra-virgin olive oil

Salt, to taste

Pepper, to taste

Crispy lettuce leaves, for serving (optional)

Instructions

In a bowl, mash together the sardines and butter or ghee with a fork. Add the mayonnaise, turmeric, onion, lemon juice, and olive oil. Mash again. Season with salt and pepper. Refrigerate for 20 to 30 minutes, or until set. Enjoy on top of crispy lettuce leaves (if using), or keep refrigerated in an airtight container for up 1 week.

Nutrition facts per serving (1 fat bomb)

Total carbs:	Fiber:	Net carbs:	Protein:	Fat:	Energy:	Calories from:
0.8 g	**0.1 g**	**0.7 g**	**5.1 g**	**17.3 g**	**178 kcal**	**Carbs (1%)** **Protein (12%)** **Fat (87%)**

Yield:
4 fat bombs

Hands-on time:
15 mins

Overall time:
**20 mins +
chilling time**

Bacon, Artichoke, and Onion Fat Bombs

Substantial enough to stand in for a full meal, these fat bombs are both delicious and sating—and they're easy to make. Stuff a rich mixture of cheese, caramelized onion, artichoke, and bacon into an avocado half, and lunch is served.

Ingredients

2 bacon slices (60 g/2.1 oz)

2 tablespoons (30 g/1.1 oz) ghee

½ large (75 g/2.6 oz) onion, peeled and diced

1 garlic clove, minced

⅓ cup (28 g/1 oz) canned artichoke hearts, sliced

¼ cup (60 g/2.1 oz) crème fraîche or sour cream

¼ cup (55 g/1.9 oz) mayonnaise, preferable homemade

1 tablespoon (15 ml/0.5 fl oz) freshly squeezed lemon juice

¼ cup (30 g/1.1 oz) grated Swiss cheese such as Gruyère

Salt, to taste

Pepper, to taste

4 medium (300 g/10.6 oz) avocado halves, pitted

Instructions

In a hot skillet, fry the bacon for a few minutes until crispy. Remove from the heat and set aside to cool. When cool enough to handle, crumble the bacon into small pieces.

Grease the same pan in which you cooked the bacon with the ghee. Add the onion and garlic and cook over medium heat until golden brown, stirring frequently to prevent burning. Set aside to cool.

In a bowl, combine the cooked onion and garlic and the artichoke hearts. Add the crème fraîche or sour cream, mayonnaise, lemon juice, grated Swiss cheese, and crumbled bacon. Mix well with a fork. Season with salt and pepper. Refrigerate for 20 to 30 minutes, or until set.

Just before serving, top each avocado half with one-quarter of the artichoke mixture and enjoy immediately. Refrigerate the artichoke mixture in an airtight container for up to 5 days.

Nutrition facts per serving (1 avocado half)

Total carbs:	Fiber:	Net carbs:	Protein:	Fat:	Energy:	Calories from:
10 g	**6 g**	**4 g**	**6.6 g**	**39.6 g**	**408 kcal**	**Carbs (4%)** **Protein (7%)** **Fat (89%)**

Yield:
4 fat bombs

Hands-on time:
15 mins

Overall time:
20 mins + chilling time

Chorizo and Avocado Fat Bombs

Load crispy bits of chorizo and diced hard-boiled eggs into avocado halves for filling fat bombs that double as a quick low-carb lunch or brunch.

Ingredients

3.5 ounces (100 g) Spanish chorizo sausage, diced

2 large hardboiled eggs, cooled, peeled, and diced

¼ cup (56 g/2 oz) unsalted butter, at room temperature

2 tablespoons (30 g/1.1 oz) mayonnaise, preferably homemade

1 tablespoon (15 ml/0.5 fl oz) freshly squeezed lemon juice

2 tablespoons (8 g/0.3 oz) chopped fresh chives

Salt, to taste

Cayenne pepper, to taste

4 large (400 g /14.1 oz) avocado halves, pitted

Instructions

In a hot pan, fry the chorizo for a few minutes until crispy. Remove from the heat and set aside.

In a mixing bowl, combine the eggs, chorizo (reserving a small amount for topping), and the butter. Mash together with a fork. Add the mayonnaise, lemon juice, and chives. Season with salt and cayenne pepper. Mix with a fork to combine. Refrigerate for 20 to 30 minutes, or until set.

Just before serving, top each avocado half with one-quarter of the egg and chorizo mixture. Sprinkle with the reserved chorizo and enjoy immediately. Keep the egg and chorizo mixture refrigerated in an airtight container for up to 5 days.

Nutrition facts per serving (1 avocado half)

Total carbs:	Fiber:	Net carbs:	Protein:	Fat:	Energy:	Calories from:
9.5 g	**6.8 g**	**2.7 g**	**11.4 g**	**38.9 g**	**419 kcal**	**Carbs (3%)** **Protein (11%)** **Fat (86%)**

About the Author

Martina Slajerova is a health and food blogger living in the United Kingdom. She holds a degree in economics and worked in auditing, but has always been passionate about nutrition and healthy living. Martina loves food, science, photography, and creating new recipes. She is a firm believer in low-carb living and regular exercise. As a science geek, she bases her views on valid research and has firsthand experience of what it means to be on a low-carb diet. Both are reflected on her blog, in her KetoDiet apps, and this book.

The KetoDiet is an ongoing project she started with her partner in 2012 and includes *The KetoDiet Cookbook*, this cookbook, and the KetoDiet apps for the iPad and iPhone (www.ketodietapp.com). When creating recipes, she doesn't focus on just the carb content: You won't find any processed foods, unhealthy vegetable oils, or artificial sweeteners in her recipes.

This book and the KetoDiet apps are for people who follow a healthy low-carb lifestyle. Martina's mission is to help you reach your goals, whether it's your dream weight or simply eating healthy food. You can find even more low-carb recipes, diet plans, and information about the keto diet on her blog: www.ketodietapp.com/blog.

Index